365 Fascinating Facts ABOUT THE

NEW TESTAMENT

D1316130

Author: Lisa Brooks

∞ 1 ∞

What Was That Reference Again?

The New Testament often quotes from the Old Testament. However, sometimes it is not clear which passage is in view, as when Matthew quoted "He [Jesus] shall be called a Nazarene" (Matthew 2:23). Jesus was from Nazareth, but no such prophecy is found in the Old Testament. It may be a wordplay from Isaiah 11:1, a Messianic prophecy referring to the "branch" (Hebrew *nezer*).

∞ 2 ∞

Hunting for the Nativity

The most popular Christian holiday is Christmas, and yet the well-known and much-beloved Christmas stories of Jesus' birth are found in only two places in the Bible: Matthew 1 and 2, and Luke 1 and 2. Mark and John, both gospels about Jesus' life, don't even mention these wonderful stories.

∞ 3 ∞

Was Jesus Born "Before Christ"?

Jesus was born sometime around the year 6 B.C. King Herod, who attempted to kill baby Jesus by killing all the Jewish male infants in and around Bethlehem, died in 4 B.C. This discrepancy is owed to the monk Dennis the Little, who in A.D. 532 came up with the idea of marking years starting with Christ's birth. Unfortunately, the year of his birth was not known until much more recently.

❧ 4 ❧

Matthew: A Jewish Gospel

The book of Matthew was written primarily for a Jewish audience. The book shows that Jesus was the Jewish Messiah, a king, and that he was descended from David and Abraham. Matthew records the story of the wise men visiting the baby Jesus, an event fitting for a king. Luke records the humbler story of the shepherds visiting Jesus.

❧ 5 ❧

Who Were the Magi?

The Greek historian Herodotus (fifth century B.C.) spoke of magi who were a priestly tribe in the Persian empire. Later (in the book of Acts), the term refers to anyone who practiced magic arts (the word "magic" comes from *magi*). The most famous magi were the wise men who visited the baby Jesus. Matthew states that they came to Bethlehem from the East (Persia, Babylonia, or Arabia).

❧ 6 ❧

The Star in the East

The nature of the famous star that guided the wise men has remained elusive. Scientific suggestions have included a comet, a new star, a supernova, or a convergence of several planets. A comet was recorded about 4 B.C., and Jupiter, Mars, and Saturn converged in the constellation Pisces in 6 B.C. Both of these events could fit the biblical story.

∞ 7 ∞

How Many Wise Men?

Tradition has it that three wise men came from the East to visit the baby Jesus. Traditionally, their names were Melchior, Gaspar, and Balthasar. In fact, the Gospel of Matthew mentions neither their names nor how many they were. The number three arose from the gifts of gold, frankincense, and myrrh that they brought.

∞ 8 ∞

Mark: An Action-Packed Gospel

Mark's account of Jesus' life is the shortest and the most action-oriented. Mark portrays Jesus as one who was constantly serving others. Mark records 18 miracles and only 4 full parables. In contrast, a much greater emphasis on Jesus' teachings is in the other gospels.

∞ 9 ∞

Unity Despite Differences

At first the Christian church was all Jewish, and Jewish tradition held that it was sinful to eat with a gentile. As the church expanded, this made some church dinners difficult. In Galatians 2:11–14, the Apostle Paul, who strongly argued for unity, gave a thorough scolding to Peter and his own partner Barnabas when they buckled to pressure from church segregationists and stopped eating with gentiles.

❧ 10 ❧

Extended Parables

Many of Jesus' parables were stories. They involved comparisons, and the characters often represented God the Father or Jesus himself. Among the most beloved extended parables are the shepherd who risks all to search for the one lost sheep, the father who eagerly takes back his wayward son, and the good Samaritan who stopped to help a robbery victim when members of society's elite would not.

❧ 11 ❧

The Eye of a Needle

Jesus used hyperbole when he said, "It is easier for a camel to go through the eye of a needle than for a rich man to enter the kingdom of God" (Mark 10:25). An unfounded tradition that this referred to a small pedestrian gate in the center of Jerusalem's wooden gates arose in the Middle Ages to soften the import of this proverb.

❧ 12 ❧

John: A Theological Gospel

The Apostle John's picture of Jesus is the most theological of the four Gospels. His focus is upon Jesus as the Son of God the Father. His book is addressed to the world at large, and his purpose was to convince people that Jesus was the Messiah, the Son of God (John 20:31). The action is slower than in Mark's Gospel, with more attention to conversations and teaching.

↬ 13 ↫

The Crucifixion of Jesus

Jesus' crucifixion followed typical Roman procedures. He was publicly whipped, forced to carry his own cross, and nailed to it. A tablet identifying him was attached above his head. Contrary to custom, however, his legs were not broken to hasten his death, since he was already dead when the soldiers came to do it. The book of John states (19:36) that this fulfilled an Old Testament prophecy.

↬ 14 ↫

Messiah: One Who Is Anointed

Our word *Messiah* comes from the Hebrew word *mashiach,* which means "anointed one." In the Old Testament, kings were anointed into their office; so any number of kings could be called messiahs. The New Testament presents Jesus as the Messiah, the one ultimate and perfect king.

↬ 15 ↫

"Abba, Father"

The Aramaic word *abba* is an intimate form of the word *ab,* which means "father." It was an informal term of intimacy and respect used by children, something like da-da or daddy. Jesus used this term in Mark 14:36 to describe the intimacy that believers could have with God the Father.

⟶ 16 ⟵

The Acts of the Apostles: After the Resurrection

The book of Acts tells the story of the early Christian church, written by Luke as a sequel to his account of Jesus. Luke showed the movement of the newly proclaimed message of Jesus Christ from its roots in Judaism and the city of Jerusalem to its transformation into a worldwide, inclusive faith that reached all the way to Rome.

⟶ 17 ⟵

Jesus, the Christ

Christ was not part of the name that Mary gave Jesus. The term is a title, and it comes from the Greek word for "messiah" (*christos*). Thus, Jesus was often referred to as "the Christ" (the Messiah). Jesus' friends would have called him *Yeshua*, the Aramaic word for Jesus.

⟶ 18 ⟵

Jesus: One Who Saves

The name Jesus (in Greek *Iesous*) is related to the Hebrew names Joshua and Isaiah, which mean "one who saves" or "Yahweh saves." The angel told Jesus' mother, Mary, to call him Jesus, because he would save his people from their sins (Matthew 1:21).

∽ **19** ∽

Not Your Ordinary Theme Park

At The Holy Land Experience in Orlando, Florida, you can experience the Word of God up close. Touted as "a living, biblical museum that takes you 7,000 miles away and 2,000 years back in time to the land of the Bible," The Holy Land Experience aims to educate and inspire through attractions such as the Garden Tomb, Jerusalem Model, and Wilderness Tabernacle. In addition, a live reenactment portraying the Crucifixion of Jesus takes place six days a week.

∽ **20** ∽

Gideon Bibles

The Gideons International have been placing Bibles in hotel rooms in the United States for more than 100 years. The organization was formed by three travelers who met in a Wisconsin hotel in 1898, and the majority of the group's early membership consisted of traveling salesmen—somewhat fitting considering that Jesus and his apostles are sometimes referred to as the greatest traveling salesmen of all time.

∞ 21 ∞

A Secret Password

The fish was an early symbol of Christianity, since the Greek word for fish, *icthus,* is an acronym for the Greek phrase *Iesous Christos Theou Huios Soter,* which means "Jesus Christ, of God the Son, Savior." It was written as graffiti, and was used as a secret password when Christians were being persecuted by the Romans.

∞ 22 ∞

1 and 2 Corinthians: Problem Solving

The church at Corinth, Greece, had many problems. Paul's letters to them—there were at least four, but only two are preserved—address their issues one by one. These issues included factions in the church, incest, marriage, food offered to idols, spiritual gifts (such as speaking in unintelligible tongues), opposition to Paul, and the concept of resurrection.

∞ 23 ∞

Galatians: Freedom from Legalism

Since all the early Christians were Jews, a question arose about Christians keeping all the Jewish laws, including circumcision. This letter was Paul's statement that Christians were made right with God only by their faith.

ꙮ 24 ꙮ

Psalms, Hymns, and Spiritual Songs

The Apostle Paul twice mentions the songs of Christian worship in his letters. He urges people to sing "psalms and hymns and spiritual songs" with great joy and thanksgiving (Ephesians 5:19; Colossians 3:16). These included the words of Scripture (psalms), as well as songs of praise (hymns) and other types of songs (spiritual songs).

ꙮ 25 ꙮ

1 and 2 Thessalonians: The End of Time

Paul gave the church at Thessalonica, Greece, encouragement and instruction in these two letters. This included much teaching about the return of Christ to earth at the end of time. This church must have had a special interest in the subject.

ꙮ 26 ꙮ

Ephesians, Philippians, Colossians: Prison Letters

The Apostle Paul spent much time in prison for his faith, and there he wrote several letters to churches. In these letters, he encouraged three different churches to know clearly what they believed and to put these beliefs into practice.

෨ **27** ෨

An Early Christian Hymn

The Apostle Paul occasionally used the words of early Christian hymns in writing his letters. The most famous example is in Philippians 2:5–11, where a soaring passage about Christ's humility, humiliation, and ultimate exaltation is found.

෨ **28** ෨

1 and 2 Timothy, Titus: Pastoral Letters

These letters were to two people who were ministers (pastors) of churches. The letters gave specific instructions about the orderly functioning of churches and for resisting false teachings.

෨ **29** ෨

Philemon: On Slavery

This is one of Paul's most intensely personal letters. It is a friendly, tactful letter to his friend Philemon, who owned a runaway slave. This slave had been captured, and he converted to Christianity under Paul in prison. Paul asked Philemon to welcome the slave as he would welcome Paul.

❧ 30 ❧

Inter-Biblical Quotes

The New Testament quotes the Old Testament hundreds of times, but only once does a New Testament author mention another New Testament writer by name. Peter cites Paul in support of his own views on God's patience in 2 Peter 3:15.

❧ 31 ❧

Hebrews: Book of Better Things

The author of this book forcefully makes the point that Jesus was the perfect fulfillment of much prophecy in the Old Testament. The book stresses the importance of faith.

❧ 32 ❧

Romans: Paul's System of Faith

The book of Romans is a letter written to Christians in Rome to explain Paul's understanding of what the Christian faith was about. This book is the most systematic and theological of his letters. The first half emphasizes the theme of righteousness and how to attain it, and the last chapters are practical exhortations about living.

↬ **33** ↫

Herod the Fox

Metaphors are figures of speech in which a term describing a certain object is used to describe something else for the purpose of making a vivid comparison. This was a rhetorical device that Jesus often used. He called King Herod "that fox" (Luke 13:32). He called himself "the bread of life" (John 6:35) and "the true vine" (John 15:1). He even called some who came to follow him "you brood of vipers!" (Luke 3:7).

↬ **34** ↫

Hagar the Mountain

An allegory is a story that carries (or gives its interpretation) a hidden meaning, or, more commonly, several hidden meanings. A well-known example is from the Apostle Paul, when he speaks of Abraham's two wives, Sarah and Hagar. He says, "Now this is an allegory: these women are two covenants. ...One woman, in fact, is Hagar, from Mount Sinai...." (Galatians 4:24–25, NRSV). He also compares Hagar with the earthly Jerusalem and Sarah with the heavenly city.

↬ **35** ↫

1 and 2 Peter: Crisis Management

The Apostle Peter's two letters offer encouragement to those suffering persecution. Peter reminds them of their fellow sufferer and the perfect example, Jesus. These letters also warn against false teachings.

∞ 36 ∞

1, 2, and 3 John:
Truth and Love

John's letters deal with truth in the face of false teaching, especially early Gnosticism (intellectual knowledge can lead to salvation). In his first letter, he also emphasizes right relationship with God through Jesus Christ, and the importance of love in all areas of our life.

∞ 37 ∞

Jude: Eclectic Warnings

This short book warns against false teachings, much in the way that 2 Peter does. A distinctive aspect of Jude is that it quotes from non-biblical books, such as the Assumption of Moses (in verse 9) and the book of Enoch (in verse 14).

∞ 38 ∞

Revelation: Visions of the End

The book of Revelation presents the Apostle John's visions of the end of time. The book is rich with symbols and strange creatures, such as angels, dragons, and beasts, great armies and cataclysmic battles, a lake of fire, and a bottomless pit. The consistent message of the book is the ultimate and final triumph of Christ over the devil and all forces of evil.

❧ 39 ❧

Beasts and Dragons

The book of Revelation is the longest example of apocalyptic literature in the Bible. It speaks of great hosts of angels and a great red dragon with seven heads and ten horns and seven crowns on its heads. It describes several beasts, one that looked like a leopard with feet like a bear's and a mouth like a lion's. The dragon and the beasts are symbols of the devil.

❧ 40 ❧

A Bold Translator

Latin was the language of the Roman empire, and so, in about A.D. 382, Pope Damasus I commissioned Jerome to produce an authoritative translation of the Bible. Jerome did, but he shocked the world by translating directly from the Hebrew text, rather than from the Greek Septuagint or earlier Latin versions, as had been the practice. His version was called the Vulgate.

❧ 41 ❧

The Oldest Greek New Testament

The oldest complete version of the New Testament is a book written on parchment dating to the fourth century A.D. It is called the Codex Sinaiticus, because it was discovered in a monastery on Mount Sinai. It was purchased from the Soviet government in 1933 by the British government for 100,000 pounds, and it is now in the British Museum in London.

☙ 42 ❧

The Shortest Verse in the Bible

The Bible's shortest verse is John 11:35, "Jesus wept." This happened when Jesus heard that his friend Lazarus had died, so he performed a miracle and brought Lazarus back from the dead.

☙ 43 ❧

The Shortest Book in the Bible

The book of 3 John is the shortest book in the Bible, with 19 fewer words than its companion book, 2 John. Both of these were about one papyrus sheet in length. Five books share the distinction of being only one chapter long: Obadiah (in the Old Testament) and Philemon, 2 John, 3 John, and Jude (in the New Testament).

☙ 44 ❧

The Most Husbands

The Sadducees told Jesus of a woman who had had seven husbands, all brothers (Matthew 22). Each one had died, and the next had married the woman. Jesus himself encountered a woman who had had five husbands, and who was currently living with a man who was not her husband (John 4).

∽ 45 ∾

The Shortest Man in the Bible

No short person's height is actually given, but Zacchaeus was noted for his short stature. Luke 19 tells us that when Jesus came to town, Zacchaeus climbed a tree to see him because he (Zacchaeus) was too short to see over the crowd. Some people joke that Job's friend Bildad the Shuhite ("shoe-height") was the world's shortest man.

∽ 46 ∾

The Smallest Seed

The smallest seed mentioned in the Bible is the tiny mustard seed. The mustard plant grew into something close to five feet tall, however. Jesus used it to characterize the growth of God's kingdom, from something small (the tiny seed) to something great (the large plant), as well as to speak of the tiny amount of faith needed to work wonders.

∽ 47 ∾

The Most Generous Person in the Bible

This honor belongs to the poor widow Jesus saw dropping two small copper coins into the treasury boxes in the Temple. These were the smallest coins in circulation, worth less than a penny, and yet they were the last things she owned. Thus, she gave "all she had to live on" (Mark 12:44).

∽ 48 ∽

Jots and Tittles

When Jesus said, "one jot or one tittle shall in no wise pass from the law, till all be fulfilled" (Matthew 5:18, KJV), he affirmed the importance of the Old Testament law. The "jot" was the *yodh,* the smallest letter of the Hebrew alphabet, while the "tittle" was only part of a letter: a small pen stroke.

∽ 49 ∽

The Language of Jesus

Aramaic, which is closely related to Hebrew, was the language that Jesus spoke. It all but died out in the centuries following Jesus' day. Amazingly, the language still survives today, but only in isolated villages in Syria, Turkey, Iraq, and Iran. Assyrian Christians from northern Iraq still speak it today as well.

∽ 50 ∽

You Devil, You!

The word "devil" comes from Greek *diablos* ("slanderer"), while "Satan" comes from Hebrew *satan* ("adversary"). The New Testament gives us most of our information about the devil, showing him as a malevolent reality, always opposed to God and his people, and whose power will be crushed in the end. He appears in many forms, such as a serpent, a dragon, a sea monster, a flash of lightning, an angel of light, and a roaring lion.

∽ 51 ∽

Beelzebub: Lord of the Flies

Beelzebub, which translates as "lord of the flies," was the name of an important Philistine god. In the New Testament, Jesus was accused of driving out demons by the power of Beelzebul (as it is spelled in the New Testament). This demon appears in William Golding's novel as an evil pig's head worshipped by choirboys-turned-savages.

∽ 52 ∽

Ancient Words of Worship

Many Hebrew or Aramaic words are used in modern-day worship. *Hallelujah* means "Praise the Lord!" *Hosanna* was a shout of acclamation used to welcome Jesus into Jerusalem, which originally meant "Save us!" *Amen* is Hebrew for "Surely! So be it!" *Maranatha* was an Aramaic word used by Paul meaning "Our Lord, come!" (referring to hopes of Christ's return to earth).

∽ 53 ∽

Greek in the Holy Land

As ancient Greece rose in power and influence toward the end of the first millennium B.C., so did its language. During the time of Jesus, it was an important language. The fact that the New Testament was written in Greek, even though most of its authors were native speakers of Aramaic, attests to the language's influence and vitality.

∽ 54 ∾

The Language of Empire and Church

John 19:20 states that the plaque on Jesus' cross was written in three languages. Hebrew was the local language, Greek was the language of commerce, and Latin was the language of the Roman Empire. When the Roman Empire became Christianized, Latin became the language of the church. In the Roman Catholic Church, Latin remained the language for Mass until the Second Vatican Council in the 1960s.

∽ 55 ∾

A Strange Meal

On two occasions, biblical characters ate a scroll that contained God's words as a symbol of internalizing them: the prophet Ezekiel (Ezekiel 2:8—3:3) and the Apostle John (Revelation 10:9–10). In both cases it tasted "sweet as honey," which echoes the words of Psalm 119:103: "How sweet are thy words to my taste, sweeter than honey to my mouth!"

∽ 56 ∾

Book Burning

The Bible records two occasions on which books were burned. King Jehoiakim of Judah burned the book of Jeremiah (Jeremiah 36:23). A number of magicians at Ephesus, who were converted as a result of Paul's preaching, brought their books of magic together and burned them publicly (Acts 19:19).

∽ 57 ∾
The Book of Life

The most commonly mentioned heavenly book is the Book of Life. It refers to the keeping of an account of those who are truly believers and those who are not. In Revelation, those whose names are found written in the Book of Life will escape the everlasting judgment. Most other heavenly books are related to the Book of Life in some way.

∽ 58 ∾
A Bible for the Commoner

The New Testament was written in the language of the common person. This style is called *koine* Greek, meaning "common," "everyday." It contrasts sharply with the sophisticated and complex Greek of Athens, called Attic Greek. This meant the New Testament could be read and understood by the vast majority of people throughout the Mediterranean world.

∽ 59 ∾
Familiar Greek Words

Many English words have their roots in Greek words used in the New Testament. *Theos* ("God") and *logos* ("word," "study") yield theology (the study of God). *Ekklesia* ("church") yields ecclesiastical (having to do with the church). *Angelos* is "angel"; *proselutos* is "proselyte"; *baptizo* is "baptize"; *meter* is "mother"; *pater* is "father."

⊙ **60** ⊙

Stammering Barbarians

Our word "barbarian" comes from the Greek *barbaros,* which referred to a foreigner, someone speaking an unintelligible language. It is found in Romans 1:14, referring to non-Greeks. The word arose to imitate the way a foreign tongue sounded to Greek ears, a stammering, unknown sound. Originally, it had no insulting connotation at all.

⊙ **61** ⊙

A Biblical Airhead

Jesus spoke about empty-headed people when he said, "And whoever says to his brother 'Raca,' shall be in danger of the council" (Matthew 5:22). The Aramaic word is one of insult, related to the Hebrew term for empty. It means something like empty-headed one (airhead or blockhead).

⊙ **62** ⊙

Paul's Thorn in the Flesh

The Apostle Paul mentioned a "thorn in the flesh" that was given him to keep him from pride (2 Corinthians 12:7). He asked God three times about it, but it was never removed. Scholars have speculated almost endlessly about what it was. Suggestions include earaches, headaches, eye afflictions, epilepsy, hysteria, malaria, speech impediment, sexual lust, or human enemies. Unfortunately, we do not know what his problem was.

☙ **63** ☙

666: The Number of the Beast

The beast's number is 666 (Revelation 13:18). This has led to endless speculation about the beast's identity. Some people have used various methods of assigning numbers to letters. Many early interpreters thought individual Roman emperors were being referred to. Being one digit short of the triple number of perfection—777—it symbolizes evil's perversion and falling short of the true standard of perfection.

☙ **64** ☙

Casting Pearls before Swine

In the Sermon on the Mount, Jesus said, "Do not give dogs what is holy; and do not throw your pearls before swine." Holy things and pearls here represent the truths of the Gospel, and dogs and pigs represent any people who have become cynical and hardened against God's word. The saying emphasized the importance of choosing how and where to preach the Gospel.

☙ **65** ☙

"Red Sky at Night, Sailors Delight"

Boy and Girl Scouts often learn such sayings to help them survive in the outdoors. However, such wisdom is not new. Jesus once told a group of Jewish leaders, "When it is evening, you say, 'It will be fair weather; for the sky is red.' And in the morning, 'It will be foul weather today, for the sky is red and threatening'" (Matthew 16:2–3).

66

Mammon

This word comes from an Aramaic term (*mamona*) meaning "wealth." Jesus gave negative connotations to the term when he said, "You cannot serve God and mammon" (Matthew 6:24) and when he referred to "unrighteous mammon" (Luke 16:9, 11). The latter term probably referred to ill-gotten gains. The point in both of these cases is as G. B. Caird said, "All money, however acquired, is tainted unless used in God's service."

67

Abraham's Bosom

The old African American spiritual that said "Rock'a my soul in the bosom of Abraham" spoke of a place of comfort and security. The phrase comes from Luke 16:22–23, in Jesus' parable about Lazarus. When Lazarus died, he was carried by the angels to "Abraham's bosom," the place of high honor and intimacy.

68

Last Words

The book of John ends with a verse which tells us that there is so much more to the story of Jesus than we know: "And there are also many other things that Jesus did, which if they were written one by one, I suppose that even the world itself could not contain the books that would be written."

᷒ **69** ᷒

Love By Any Other Name

The Greek language has three major words for love. The first (*eros*) denotes sexual love. This word was common in classical Greek, but is never found in the New Testament. The second (*philos*) denotes married love or a close friendship. The third (*agape*) was rarely used in classical Greek, but it is the most common word for love in the New Testament. The biblical writers used it to depict God's love.

᷒ **70** ᷒

Theopneustos: A New Word

An example where Paul actually invented a new word is *Theopneustos,* which means "God-breathed." This is formed by combining *Theos* ("God") and *pneuma* ("breath"). The word was not used in Paul's day, but he coined the term to describe the nature of Scripture: It was "God-breathed," meaning the very words of God (2 Timothy 3:16). Usually *Theopneustos* is translated "inspired by God."

᷒ **71** ᷒

What's That Log Doing in Your Eye?

Jesus used hyperbole and figurative language very effectively when he scolded people for noticing specks or splinters in other people's eyes while ignoring the logs in their own eyes (Matthew 7:3–5). His point was to condemn hypocrisy.

72

"Get behind Me, Satan!"

This is the rebuke Jesus directed at Peter when he was speaking of the suffering that Jesus was to undergo, and Peter objected that this should not occur (Matthew 16:23). The effect of Peter's words was to tempt Jesus to abandon his mission, and he rebuked Peter in similar terms that he had done earlier with Satan himself (Matthew 4:10). The phrase is now used in a joking manner, when innocent temptations arise.

73

Turning the Other Cheek

In Jesus' Sermon on the Mount, he spoke in detail about ethical living. He stated that if someone "slaps you on your right cheek, turn the other to him also" (Matthew 5:39). This made the point about not seeking revenge for injury, but forgiving wrongdoers.

74

Through a Glass Darkly

The Apostle Paul spoke of heavenly things using this eloquent phrase. In the King James Version, he said that we perceive heavenly things imperfectly, as "through a glass, darkly; but then face to face" (1 Corinthians 13:12). Modern versions speak of seeing in a mirror dimly, but the point is the same.

∽ 75 ∾

The Sign of Jonah

When the Pharisees and Sadducees asked Jesus for a sign, he refused, except to refer them to "the sign of the prophet Jonah" (Matthew 12:39). Just as Jonah had been in the fish's belly for three days and nights, so Jesus would be in the grave for the same amount of time. Jesus' appearance after the three days would indict his generation, just as Jonah's appearance in Nineveh after three days indicted the Ninevites.

∽ 76 ∾

Whitewashed Tombs

A striking metaphor that Jesus used was to compare the Pharisees with whitewashed tombs to show their hypocrisy. On the outside, many of them were freshly painted and clean, but on the inside they were full of dead bones and all manner of uncleanness.

∽ 77 ∾

Jesus and the U.S. Marines

The U.S. Marine Corps had a recruiting slogan that said they were looking for "a few good men." This is similar to Jesus' words about the relatively few people who would actually respond to his invitation to salvation—"many are called, but few are chosen" (Matthew 22:14). The major difference is that the Marines' invitation was exclusive, while Jesus' was inclusive.

∽ **78** ∾

Speaking in Tongues

On the day of Pentecost, Jesus' followers were together in a house when a mighty wind rushed upon them, flames of fire rested on each of them, and they each began to "speak in tongues" (in languages they did not know). Jews from many different countries were in Jerusalem at the time, and each heard Jesus' followers speaking in their own language. This was a sign of the Holy Spirit's presence.

∽ **79** ∾

Physician, Heal Thyself

This was a skeptical challenge that Jesus predicted the people from his hometown would hurl at him when he tried to do miracles there. It could be paraphrased as follows: You heal others so well, let's see you heal yourself. Jesus called it a proverb, indicating that it must have been a common phrase. The attitude it expresses is "you have done so well elsewhere, let's see you do the same here."

∽ **80** ∾

Who Was Belial?

Belial was not originally a name, but it developed into a name for Satan in Jewish literature in the period between the Testaments. The Apostle Paul used the word in this way when he asked "What accord has Christ with Belial?" (2 Corinthians 6:15).

81

"Away in a Manger"

The Gospel of Luke mentions the manger into which Jesus was laid when he was born (Luke 2:7). Most scholars think this was a feeding trough for cattle. Excavations at Megiddo and Lachish, towns of the Old Testament period, have uncovered stone feeding troughs of this type. St. Jerome stated that Jesus' manger was made of mud or clay, which may be true given the scarcity of wood and the difficulty of hewing out stone.

82

Thirty Pieces of Silver

The price paid to Judas for Jesus was 30 pieces of silver. This was a ridiculously low sum. In the Old Testament, this was the sum to be paid if a man's ox gored a slave. This reflects the low esteem in which Jesus was held by Judas and the Jewish leaders.

83

Faith, Hope, and Love

Paul's great reflections on love are found in 1 Corinthians 13. At the end of his discussion, he stresses that "faith, hope, and love" are the greatest of all gifts, but he concludes that "the greatest of these is love."

∞ 84 ∞

Kings and Donkeys

Several passages in the Old Testament speak of a king riding on a donkey. This is most striking in Zechariah 9:9, where it is prophesied that a king comes triumphant and victorious yet riding humbly on a donkey. Jesus' entrance into Jerusalem on a donkey fulfilled this prophecy (Matthew 21:5). The use of a donkey instead of a horse emphasized the peaceful nature of the king.

∞ 85 ∞

Judge Not

In Matthew 7:1, Jesus says, "Judge not, that you be not judged." This text is not meant to be a diatribe against all discernment. It's a warning against hypocrisy, criticizing others for the things we're doing.

∞ 86 ∞

Dragons

Dragons are found in both the Old and New Testaments. In the Old Testament, the term is sometimes more accurately translated as serpent, but often it refers to the great monster of mythology. It is a symbol of evil. In Revelation 12, it is a symbol of Satan. Dragons are known from the literature and art of the ancient Near East as well.

∽ **87** ∾

Snake Handlers

Mark 16 states that just before Jesus returned to heaven, he told his followers that they would have new powers because of their faith: They would be able to cast out demons, speak in new languages, handle deadly snakes, and drink poison with no harm. Some eccentric Christian groups today, mainly in Appalachia, take this to mean that all Christians *must* do this, and they handle snakes and drink poisons as part of their religious rituals.

∽ **88** ∾

Saint Peter's Fish

Jesus told his disciple Peter to go fish in the Sea of Galilee, predicting that the first fish he caught would have a shekel coin in its mouth (Matthew 17:24–27). Peter was then to take this shekel to pay his and Jesus' taxes with it. The fish was probably the Tilapia, a fish commonly found in the Sea of Galilee. This fish has a large mouth in which it carries its eggs, and it is often called St. Peter's Fish.

∽ **89** ∾

Roosters

In the New Testament, Mark 13:35 mentions "cockcrow" as the signal for morning. The only other reference is to the cock that crowed when Peter denied Jesus.

∽ 90 ∾
Scorpions

Scorpions are mentioned many times in the Bible, always as threats the Israelites faced or as symbols of great pain and hardship. Jesus appointed 70 followers to whom he gave authority to "trample on serpents and scorpions . . . and nothing shall by any means hurt you" (Luke 10:19).

∽ 91 ∾
Jesus' Sponge

Roman soldiers gave Jesus a drink from a sponge while he was on the cross. Sponges are marine animals whose skeletons provide the familiar sponge. The Roman writer Pliny states that it was standard practice for Roman soldiers to carry a sponge with them to use in getting themselves a drink, precisely in the way that the Gospels describe.

∽ 92 ∾
Paul and the Lion's Mouth

The Apostle Paul stated once that he was "delivered out of the mouth of the lion" (2 Timothy 4:17). Some see this as a reference to a lion in a Roman amphitheater. However, it comes in a context where Paul is speaking of opposition to him, and so others see a reference to the devil here. This is perhaps more likely, since the devil is spoken of as "a roaring lion, seeking whom he may devour" (1 Peter 5:8).

∽ **93** ∽

The Four Horsemen of the Apocalypse

Revelation 6 mentions four magnificent horses and their riders, representing the evils to come at the end of the world. The first horse was white, representing conquest; the second, red, representing war; the third, black, representing famine. The fourth horse was pale, its rider's name was Death. It represented war, famine, pestilence, and wild beasts all at once.

∽ **94** ∽

The Judas Tree

This is the name given to a tree that Judas supposedly hung himself from (Matthew 27:5). It has reddish flowers that look like drops of blood. The flowers appear before the leaves, and spring straight out of the trunk itself. The tree is the *Cercis siliquastrum.* Tradition states that the tree weeps blood each spring in memory of Judas.

∽ **95** ∽

Sycamore Trees

The prophet Amos was a "tender of sycamore fruit" by profession (Amos 7:14). The figs of the sycamore tree require cutting open with a knife point at a certain stage to help in the ripening process, and Amos did this. Branches of the sycamore tree are strong and wide-spreading, and Zacchaeus climbed such a tree in order to see Jesus better (Luke 19:4).

96

C. S. Lewis's Wormwood

In C. S. Lewis's fictional book *The Screwtape Letters*, about the correspondence between two devils, one devil is named Wormwood. His job is to poison the mind of the human being assigned to him. This imagery is taken from Revelation 8:8–11 where a star named Wormwood fell from heaven and poisoned the waters on earth.

97

Jesus and the Temple

Jesus freely came and went in the Temple and its courtyards. Under the colonnades of the outer court, the Jewish scribes and Pharisees taught the Law and held their debates. It was here that the 12-year-old Jesus impressed these rabbis with his knowledge. It was also here that an angry Jesus overturned the tables of the moneychangers and the merchants because they had turned God's house into "a den of thieves."

98

Grave Robbers Beware!

In 1878, a Greek inscription labeled as an "Ordinance of Caesar" was brought to Europe, probably from Nazareth. Many scholars date it to about A.D. 50. It was 20 lines long and it proclaimed capital punishment for anyone who violated a grave in any way. This was an unusual feature of Roman law at this time.

∞ **99** ∞

Jesus' Tomb and the Nazareth Decree

If the Ordinance of Caesar (also known as the Nazareth Decree) dates to A.D. 50, then the emperor Claudius issued it some 20 years after Jesus' death and resurrection. Some Jews said that Jesus' body was stolen from the grave (Matthew 28:11–15), so Claudius' decree may have been in reaction to this story. If so, it is the first extra-biblical indication that the Roman government was aware of Jesus.

∞ **100** ∞

Nativity Scene

There is no stable or innkeeper in the nativity story. The Greek word for "inn" usually referred to the guest room of a house. It's likely that the animals were kept in an adjoining room or perhaps in a courtyard under the guest room, and the manger would be there.

∞ **101** ∞

The Parables of Jesus

Jesus' favorite teaching tool was the parable. In its simplest form, the parable uses a comparison to make a point. It is simple, direct, and the point is clear, such as "The kingdom of heaven is like treasure hidden in a field, which a man found and hid; and for joy over it he goes and sells all that he has and buys that field" (Matthew 13:44).

102

Pentecost: Early Harvest Feast

This feast comes 50 days after the first Sabbath of Passover—*pent* means 50. It was a spring festival celebrating the completion of the grain harvest. Acts 2 tells us that Christians received the Holy Spirit on the day of Pentecost and spoke in languages not their own. Today, Pentecostals are Christians who practice speaking in tongues.

103

Sunday: The Christian Sabbath?

Most Christians celebrate Sunday as a day of rest. This is to remind them of Jesus' resurrection from the dead on that day. For many Christians, this choice of day is also a conscious rejection of what they regard as Old Testament ritual law, which Christians are no longer subject to. Other Christians do celebrate the Sabbath on Saturday, to remind them of the Old Testament Sabbath day.

104

The Body and Blood of Christ

Christians celebrate the sacrificial death of Christ by eating and drinking bread and wine. The broken bread symbolizes Christ's broken body and the wine symbolizes his shed blood. Some Christians believe that these elements actually become the body and blood of Christ when a priest blesses them during the ceremony of the Eucharist (or mass).

∞ 105 ∞

Palm Sunday

In Christian tradition, the Sunday before Easter has come to be known as Palm Sunday. This was because people welcomed Jesus into Jerusalem by spreading leafy branches on the road before his donkey as he was entering the city at the time of the Passover (in the spring). The cutting of palm branches was usually practiced in the fall, at the Festival of Tabernacles, as part of the construction of the booths (Leviticus 23:40–42).

∞ 106 ∞

The Holy Grail

The cup supposedly used by Jesus at the Last Supper with his disciples became the subject of many legends. At King Arthur's Round Table, an empty seat was reserved for the knight who found the Grail. In the early twentieth century, an ancient silver cup was publicized as being the Holy Grail, but is usually dated no earlier than the fourth century A.D.

∞ 107 ∞

Pilate's Hand Washing

The Roman governor Pilate washed his hands at Jesus' arraignment to symbolize his withdrawal from responsibility for whatever might happen to Jesus (Matthew 27:24). This practice was not new. The Old Testament has many examples of ritual hand washing to symbolize innocence (Psalm 26:6 and Deuteronomy 21:6–8).

∞ **108** ∞

Foot Washing

Since people wore sandals in dusty Bible lands, their feet had to be washed frequently. This is mentioned several times in the Old Testament (see Genesis 18:4). Not washing one's feet was a sign of mourning (2 Samuel 19:24). It was considered to be the work of a slave, but Jesus washed his disciples' feet in order to emphasize the necessity of serving others (John 13).

∞ **109** ∞

A Cross to Bear

The expression "That's a cross I have to bear" comes from Jesus' words in Matthew 16:24: "If anyone desires to come after Me, let him deny himself, and take up his cross, and follow Me." Prisoners condemned to death by crucifixion often were forced to carry their own crossbeam—it was a sign of impending death.

∞ **110** ∞

How Long Was Jesus Dead?

The total time Jesus was dead was not much more than 36 hours. According to the Gospels, Jesus died on a Friday afternoon, about 3:00 p.m. He was placed in a tomb that evening and remained there until sometime early Sunday morning, before the women got there. The popular notion of three days comes from the Jewish way of counting days, in which any portion of a day counts as a full day.

☙ 111 ☙

Patience Is a Virtue

In 1 Thessalonians, Paul speaks of Jesus' return. Scholars suspect that some of the Thessalonian Christians took Paul's words about the "rapture" too far, quitting their jobs or taking other drastic measures to await the Lord's return. So it makes sense that Paul's second letter to this church mentions signs that will precede Jesus' coming (2 Thessalonians 2:1–12).

☙ 112 ☙

The Athenians' Unknown God

When Paul was in Athens, he tried to establish a point of reference with his pagan audience by telling them that he had seen one of their altars dedicated "To an unknown god" (Acts 17:23). He then told them that the God he was preaching about was this unknown god. Later extra-biblical references, including a partially broken inscription, confirm the existence of altars of unknown gods at Athens.

☙ 113 ☙

Artemis' Sacred Stone

One of the Seven Wonders of the Ancient World was the Temple of Artemis (Diana) at Ephesus. Paul's preaching against idolatry at Ephesus threatened the lucrative trade in religious souvenirs, since people came from all around to see the temple and "the image which fell down from Zeus" (Acts 19:35). Perhaps this was a meteor that landed there.

∞ 114 ∞

The Ruler of the Synagogue

This was an official who presided over the board of elders of the synagogue. Sometimes the entire board of elders was considered to be the "rulers," as when Paul and Barnabas received permission to preach from the rulers of the synagogue at Antioch (Acts 13:15). Their authority included the power to discipline and even to excommunicate people.

∞ 115 ∞

The Sanhedrin

The Sanhedrin is much better known than the "Great Synagogue" as the supreme Jewish law council. It is mentioned several times in the New Testament, usually referring to Jesus' trial (where it is called the council). The Sanhedrin consisted of 70 members, plus a head (high priest), and Jewish tradition traces its origins back to the council of 70 elders that Moses appointed in the wilderness (Numbers 11:16).

∞ 116 ∞

"Let Your Yes Be Yes"

This expression comes from Jesus' words in the Sermon on the Mount, when he stated that people should not swear falsely, nor should they take any oaths by heaven or by Jerusalem or by anything else. A simple yes or no should be binding. The King James Version says "let your communication be, Yea, yea; Nay, nay" (Matthew 5:37).

∞ **117** ∞

Too Much Praying?

While prayer was to be practiced at any time, even unceasingly, it was to be done meaningfully. Jesus warned about idly and endlessly repeating empty phrases in prayer (Matthew 6:7). One Jewish rabbi went to the extreme of stating that Jews should not pray every hour of the day, so that they would not get into the habit of calling on God mindlessly, thus leading to disrespect.

∞ **118** ∞

The Temptation of Christ

The book of Hebrews states that Jesus, even though he was God, was tempted to sin just as we are, but he was able to resist the temptation (4:15). This is part of an argument that he identifies with our struggles. The Bible says nothing about the normal temptations he probably faced growing up, but it does record the three temptations by Satan at the beginning of his public ministry (Matthew 4).

∞ **119** ∞

A Naked Escape

The Gospel of Mark is the only one of the four gospels to mention the episode of a young man who escaped naked from the Garden of Gethsemane at Jesus' arrest (Mark 14:51–52). The details seem too autobiographical for the reference to not be the book's author—Mark himself.

☙ 120 ☙

Water Baptism

Baptism with water was an integral part of the early Christians' lives. Peter preached, "Repent, and let every one of you be baptized . . . for the remission of sins" (Acts 2:38). Jewish custom stressed ritual washings, but baptism was really a Christian development.

☙ 121 ☙

The Baptism of the Holy Spirit

Several times Jesus prophesied about a baptism that would come from the Holy Spirit. John the Baptist stated that his baptism was with water, but Jesus' was different: "He will baptize you with the Holy Spirit and fire" (Matthew 3:11). Paul spoke of all believers being "baptized into one body" by one Spirit (1 Corinthians 12:13). This means that Christians would be filled and covered with the Spirit as they were covered by water in baptism.

☙ 122 ☙

Paul and Adoption

Adoption was common in Roman culture. Under Roman law, the adoptee left his old status and entered into a new relationship with his new father. He had the rights and responsibilities of any natural-born children. Paul used this imagery to portray what happens to new believers: They are adopted into God's family as his own children (Romans 8).

∽ 123 ∾

Christian Head Coverings

Christian tradition follwed Greek custom: Men's heads were not to be covered during worship (1 Corinthians 11:4). Indeed, this was a sign of dishonor to God. Women, however, were to have their heads covered as a sign of honor (11:5–6). Scholars disagree whether Paul meant that a woman's head covering was to be a veil or shawl, or merely long hair.

∽ 124 ∾

The New Covenant

The New Testament speaks about the new covenant that God made with his people. Even the term "New Testament" means new covenant. The Old Testament mentions the new covenant by name once, in Jeremiah 31:31: "Behold, the days are coming, says the Lord, when I will make a new covenant with the house of Israel and the house of Judah."

∽ 125 ∾

The Staff of Life

The term "staff of life" refers to a dietary staple, such as bread. Bread was the staff of life in the ancient Near East. The phrase probably comes from Leviticus 26:26, which mentions the "staff of bread." The word *bread* is often used for food in the Bible. This is why, in John 6:35, Jesus refers to himself as "the bread of life."

∽ 126 ∾
The Key of David

Eliakim was made the grand vizier over the household of King Hezekiah (Isaiah 22:15–25). He was given "the key of the house of David" to wear on his shoulder. This symbolized his exclusive authority to grant access to the king. This image is picked up in Revelation 3:7, where Christ now has "the key of David," and he alone now grants access to God.

∽ 127 ∾
Peter's Keys

Jesus told Peter that "I will give you the keys of the kingdom of heaven, and whatever you bind on earth will be bound in heaven" (Matthew 16:19). This was a statement of the authority he received. The Roman Catholic tradition has held that this authority was exclusively Peter's, and, through him, the Church's. Protestant traditions have held that Peter represents the Apostles, and the authority refers to the wider apostolic message and mission.

∽ 128 ∾
Durable Roman Aqueducts

The Romans constructed magnificent aqueduct systems. Jerusalem's aqueducts brought water into the city from as far away as 25 miles. These aqueducts were refurbished and used in many later periods, including under the British mandate in 1918.

∞ 129 ∞

Mint, Dill, and Cumin

These were green herbs mentioned by Jesus in his condemnation of many Pharisees' hypocrisy (Matthew 23:23). He said that they scrupulously gave a tenth of their supply of these herbs to God, in legalistic observance of the law, but that they neglected the more important things, such as justice, mercy, and faithfulness.

∞ 130 ∞

Ancient Popularity

After the New Testament, of which there are approximately 25,000 ancient copies in existence, the second most common ancient text in existence is Homer's Iliad, with 643 known copies.

∞ 131 ∞

The Galilee Boat

Jesus spent much of his time around the Sea of Galilee and even on fishing boats in the sea. In 1985, such a boat from Jesus' time was recovered from the mud of the seabed, which was exposed during a drought. The boat would have been rowed by four men, could hold up to 15 men, and could easily have accommodated Jesus and his disciples.

⊚ 132 ⊚

What's a Talent?

The talents in Jesus' parable of the master who gave his servants several talents were units of money. These were enormous sums of money, since the Greek *talanton* weighed between 57 and 95 pounds, and one talent was more than 15 years wages for a laborer. The modern English meaning of talent as ability was derived by expanding the meaning of the Greek word in this parable.

⊚ 133 ⊚

The Ephesus Theater

Acts 19 mentions a riot instigated by the Apostle Paul's presence at Ephesus, which spilled over into the great Roman theater there. This theater is typical of the countless fine Roman and Greek theaters built throughout Mediterranean lands. These theaters held large crowds but still had perfect sight lines for the audience and were models of good acoustics.

⊚ 134 ⊚

Stoning

Stoning was a form of ritual execution for certain proscribed crimes. These crimes included sacrificing a child to the god Molech, practicing witchcraft, blaspheming God's holy name, and leading people astray to worship other gods. Stoning was also a product of mob violence: Paul was stoned and left for dead at Lystra (Acts 14:19).

∞ 135 ∞

Salt That Has Lost Its Flavor

This expression comes from Jesus, who compared his disciples to salt and their uselessness if they lost their "flavor," their commitment to Christ (Mark 9:50). Sodium chloride is usually a stable compound. However, most salt in Palestine came from the Dead Sea, where other minerals and sand were mixed with it. The salt could dissolve, leaving a tasteless compound.

∞ 136 ∞

Crucifixion: Cruel and Unusual Punishment

Crucifixion was normally reserved for the lower classes in Greek and Roman societies. It was a humiliating and excruciatingly slow, painful death. Prisoners were normally whipped until blood flowed, then they were either tied or nailed to the cross and left to die of gradual suffocation.

∞ 137 ∞

Early Christians, Churches, and the Synagogue

Today's Christian worship service owes its origins to the synagogue service. Jesus himself attended and taught in the synagogue (Luke 4:16–21). The apostles Peter and John went to the Temple to pray (Acts 3:1), and the Apostle Paul regularly went to synagogues first when he arrived in a city.

∽ **138** ∾

An Impressive Engineering Feat

King Herod's greatest project in Jerusalem involved the Temple and its supporting platform. The Temple hill was sloped on all sides, so Herod had large terraces constructed to enlarge the platform. The Temple Mount measured roughly 984 feet by 1,640 feet (300 meters by 500 meters), and in some places the height of the walls reached a little over 164 feet (50 meters)!

∽ **139** ∾

Care for the Dead

Dead bodies were well cared for in all ancient societies. In the New Testament, we see examples of corpses being washed, anointed with aromatic preparations, and wrapped in linen cloths or bandages with a separate face cloth. Lack of burial was the ultimate humiliation. The evil queen Jezebel was left in the street and her flesh eaten by the dogs.

∽ **140** ∾

Ancient Ephesus

Archaeologists have dug up portions of the wealthy district of Ephesus. Some homes had heated bathrooms with running water. A brothel and casino were found in the center of town.

∞ 141 ∞

The True Morning Star

Christ is the true "morning star" in the New Testament. He is called this in 2 Peter 1:19 ("the morning star rises in your hearts") and Revelation 22:16 ("I am the Root and the Offspring of David, the Bright and Morning Star"). These allusions pick up on such Old Testament passages as Numbers 24:17: "A Star shall come out of Jacob."

∞ 142 ∞

The Angel Gabriel

Gabriel is mentioned only four times in the Bible. Twice he appeared to Daniel to teach him things beyond his comprehension. In the New Testament, Gabriel announced to Zechariah the priest the coming birth of his son, John the Baptist, and he announced to Mary the coming birth of Jesus. *Gabriel* means "God is mighty" or "mighty man of God."

∞ 143 ∞

Michael, the Archangel

Michael is an archangel who disputed with Satan in Jude 1:9. Michael's role was less a messenger (such as Gabriel) and more an angelic defender who led armies of angels against the forces of evil. In Revelation 12:7, Michael and his angels fought the great, evil dragon and its forces.

∽ **144** ∽

Herodium: A Man-Made Mountain

In 23 B.C., King Herod built a spectacular palace-fortress complex for himself in the wilderness southeast of Jerusalem. A 90-foot-high cylindrical double wall was constructed around the top of a natural hill, and then a sloping fill of earth and gravel added around it, partially burying the wall. This created an impregnable cone-shaped mountain that is visible from Jerusalem, eight miles away. Herod is buried at Herodium, but his tomb has never been discovered.

∽ **145** ∽

An Ancient City

Jerusalem was greatly ancient even by the time of Christ, with known habitation at least back to 3000 B.C. It had already been fought over, conquered, destroyed, and rebuilt numerous times. It was one of the Holy Land's most cosmopolitan cities and a center of Roman administration, and its permanent population was somewhere between 30,000-50,000.

∽ **146** ∽

Superstition

The book of Revelation states that 666 is the Mark of the Beast, or Antichrist. According to store clerks, many superstitious people will add a small item to their purchases if the total comes out to $6.66, so they can avoid paying this frightening sum. In fact, it apparently happens quite often!

∽ 147 ∾

Artistic License

If you look closely at Leonardo da Vinci's famous painting *The Last Supper*, you'll see oranges. It turns out that da Vinci took some creative license. According to horticultural experts, oranges weren't grown in the Holy Land until long after Jesus' time.

∽ 148 ∾

Duodecimal Disciples

The number 12 has significance in the Bible. It refers to the 12 tribes of Israel, and also to the 12 apostles: Simon Peter, Andrew, James and his brother John, Philip, Bartholomew, Thomas, Matthew, James, Thaddaeus, Simon, and Judas Iscariot. What a motley crew they were. Fishers, a tax collector, a former terrorist: Would you entrust your whole life's work to any of them?

∽ 149 ∾

The Second Temple

The Temple that Jesus knew was first built in 516 B.C., but it was greatly expanded by King Herod and his successors into a magnificent structure with many impressive courtyards, chambers, colonnades, and gates around it. The finished product took more than 80 years to complete. Jesus had foreseen that it would be destroyed.

∽ 150 ∽

An Anonymous Letter

Most New Testament letter writers identify themselves. Only one—Hebrews—departs from this norm. Foregoing greetings, it dives right into its teachings. And is it coincidence that the only unidentified New Testament author wrote the Bible's premier chapter on faith? Hebrews 11 begins, "Now faith is the substance of things hoped for, the evidence of things not seen." It does make you think!

∽ 151 ∽

Handel's *Messiah*

One of the most well-known classical choral pieces comes from George Frideric Handel's *Messiah*. Known as the "Hallelujah Chorus," this song has stirred audiences since its debut in 1742. The "Hallelujah Chorus" comes from a vision of God's final victory in Revelation 19:6: "And I heard, as it were, the voice of a great multitude...saying, 'Alleluia! For the Lord God Omnipotent reigns!'"

∽ 152 ∽

Prolific Writing

The New Testament was originally written in Greek. Nearly 5,650 handwritten copies survive in the original language and around 10,000 copies in Latin. When you throw in other languages, a total of approximately 25,000 ancient copies of the New Testament are still in existence.

∞ 153 ∞

Does the Punishment Fit the Crime?

A relatively common ancient death penalty was stoning. Acts 7 mentions that Stephen was stoned for preaching the Gospel to an angry mob. And a passage in Hebrews 11 describes another terrible punishment: being cut in two. That must have been fairly slow and very unpleasant, to say the least.

∞ 154 ∞

Going the Extra Mile

In the Sermon on the Mount, Jesus spoke repeatedly about going beyond the minimal requirements of law or social courtesy in order to show true generosity of spirit. One vivid illustration was when he said, "whoever compels you to go one mile, go with him two" (Matthew 5:41). This referred to a detested Roman practice of forcing civilians into the service of carrying military baggage for a prescribed distance, one Roman mile.

∞ 155 ∞

Luke: Beloved Physician's Gospel

Luke was the only Gentile among the New Testament's authors, and he wrote for a Gentile audience. As a medical doctor, he tells us that he investigated his subject matter thoroughly before setting forth his account (Luke 1:1–4), and his eye for details is evident. His book also has a warm, human touch to it.

∞ 156 ∞
Biblical Sports

In 1 Corinthians 9:24–27, Paul speaks of physical training and running races. The people of the Bible were very much like us, and they enjoyed the competition and fellowship of participating in contests that challenged them physically and mentally. Some biblical archaeological studies refer to ancient sports and recreation. These included primitive versions of soccer, cricket, field hockey, and a baseball-like game called round ball.

∞ 157 ∞
Immanuel: God with Us

One of the most famous prophecies about the Messiah is found in Isaiah 7:14, where a virgin is to conceive and bear a son named Immanuel. This name is *Imma-nu-el* in Hebrew, literally translated it means "with us (is) God." Matthew 1:23 quotes this as having been fulfilled in Jesus.

∞ 158 ∞
Book of Contrasts

The Bible is an exercise in dichotomy. For example, various passages talk of Jesus as God, such as John 1:1 and Romans 9:5, while others specifically address his humanity. Among the latter: John 1:14, Luke 2:7, and Hebrews 4:15.

☙ 159 ❧

Lesson Learned

In the early days of the Christian movement, people were selling their property and donating to the church. One couple, Ananias and Sapphira, decided to do the same, but held back some of the proceeds. When Ananias made the donation, fudging the numbers, he was struck dead. A few hours later, his wife came in, repeated the lie, and she dropped dead too. The stern lesson for believers: Don't lie to God.

☙ 160 ❧

An Unusual Escape

Saul, an opponent of the church, was on his way to arrest Christians in Damascus, but he was converted. Now his former colleagues were plotting to kill him. Normal escape routes were too dangerous, so Saul's new friends "took him by night and let him down through an opening in the wall, lowering him in a basket" (Acts 9:25). After that, Saul (later known as Paul) rushed off to Jerusalem and decades of effective ministry.

☙ 161 ❧

Pilate's Inscription

Various Jewish and Roman historians mentioned Pontius Pilate, but if there was any doubt about his existence, it was answered in 1961 when a stone plaque was found in Caesarea bearing his name, with the title, "prefect of Judea."

∞ 162 ∞

Fishing Nets

The New Testament mentions different types of nets used in fishing. These include the small cast net that was thrown out by hand, and the large drag net that was several hundred yards long and whose two ends were laboriously hauled into shore. Many of Jesus' disciples were fishermen, and the Bible also mentions the work of maintaining the nets, including washing (Luke 5:2), spreading and drying (Ezekiel 47:10), and mending (Matthew 4:21).

∞ 163 ∞

Biblical Capernaum

This city was a relatively young city in Jesus' day, established sometime around 200 B.C. It lasted over a thousand years before dying out in roughly A.D. 1050. Fishing and agriculture were the main activities. It was never a wealthy place; it had few luxurious houses. It did have a Roman tax office, so it wasn't insignificant. If it weren't for Jesus, however, Capernaum would be just another ancient ruin on the Sea of Galilee.

∞ 164 ∞

Thou Shalt Not Steal

Although God is pretty clear that theft is condemned, not everybody seems to have gotten the message. According to bookstore statistics, the Bible is by far the most shoplifted book in the United States!

∽ 165 ∽

Did Jesus Have a Bar Mitzvah?

At the age of 12, Jesus traveled with his family to Jerusalem where he met with rabbis. Many readers assume that this was his *bar mitzvah*, a Hebrew term for "son of the commandment." In Judaism today, when a boy turns 13, a ceremony is held declaring him an adult. However, the custom of a bar mitzvah arose only a few centuries ago. So it's unlikely that Jesus' boyhood journey involved such a ceremony.

∽ 166 ∽

Child's Play

Quite a few children's toys have been unearthed among the ruins of ancient Israelite towns. These include whistles, rattles, marbles, dolls, and toy animals. Israelite children also kept pets, such as birds. Of course, children were expected to help out in the house, farm, or family business, but when they weren't working they danced, sang, and played games in the streets.

∽ 167 ∽

A Day's Work

Most people know that Jesus was a carpenter, but what did that involve? Carpenters and woodworkers made homes, tools for farming, and weapons for war. The word used for this trade could refer to other artisans as well. Some became metal workers, shaping tools, weapons, and jewelry.

∞ **168** ∞

Everything in Moderation

Wine was the most common drink besides water in the ancient Near East. While drunkenness is acknowledged as a problem in Ephesians 5:18, wine is generally seen in the Bible as something positive, marking joyous celebrations and solemn religious occasions alike. Jesus' first recorded miracle, at the wedding of Cana, was to turn water into wine.

∞ **169** ∞

Ancient Baths

Washing and bathing were done in all biblical periods for religious and health reasons. The Greeks and Romans introduced large public baths, and many remains of these baths have been found throughout the Mediterranean region. Archaeologists believe a ritual bath facility adjoined the Temple complex in Jerusalem in Jesus' time. That way worshippers could prepare themselves.

∞ **170** ∞

The First Potluck?

In the first centuries of the Church, communion, or the Lord's Supper, was celebrated within the context of a meal. That meal was an "agape meal," or "love feast." When the Apostle Paul describes this meal in 1 Corinthians 11, it is clear that the various participants are each bringing food.

⟋ **171** ⟍

Medieval Copyists

In the years before scanners and photocopiers, how were Bibles copied? Very carefully. Jewish scribes and Christian monks painstakingly reproduced page after page by hand, with stringent rules to preserve the accuracy of the text. During the Middle Ages, copying became an art form, with elaborate calligraphy and colored inks used in manuscripts.

⟋ **172** ⟍

The First Christians

It makes sense: A Christian is a follower of Christ. *Christ* is the Greek form of the Hebrew term *messiah*, so more specifically, a Christian is one who believes Jesus is the promised Messiah of the Hebrew scriptures. But it took a while for Jesus' followers to take on the name of "Christians." It wasn't until they established a church outside Jerusalem, in Antioch of Syria, that they became known as Christians (Acts 11:26).

⟋ **173** ⟍

A Second Chance?

In 1 Peter 3:19, the author speaks of Jesus preaching "to the spirits in prison" between his own death and resurrection. This verse came to be interpreted as an indication that Jesus preached the gospel to those who had died before his coming, giving them an opportunity to believe and be released from hell.

❧ 174 ❧
The Western Wall

In Jesus' day, the temple in Jerusalem reached up to 90 feet. No part of the temple exists today, except for an outer wall that surrounded the courtyard of the temple. The Romans did not destroy this section of the wall in part because it was not part of the temple itself. Today it is known most frequently as the "Western Wall" or the "Wailing Wall."

❧ 175 ❧
Jesus and the Queen of the South

In the New Testament, the queen of Sheba is called "the queen of the South" (Sheba was probably in southern Arabia). Jesus referred to her, saying that she had come a long distance to honor Solomon. The implication was that Jesus, being greater than Solomon, was worthy of even greater honor. Jesus said she would arise at the judgment to condemn the evil generation that rejected him (Jesus) instead of honoring him (Luke 11:31).

❧ 176 ❧
A Rome by Any Other Name

In the book of Revelation, John paints a picture of a corrupt, bloodthirsty Rome. However, he does not refer to Rome by name, thus avoiding any charge of insurrection by the Roman authorities. Instead, he names Babylon, but readers during his day would comprehend the true identity of "Babylon."

∞ 177 ∞

Thomas, "the Twin"

The name Thomas means "the twin" in Aramaic. A natural question for us to ask is, the twin of whom? An unusual tradition in Syria said that this Thomas was actually the twin brother of Jesus. A more likely explanation seems to come from the third-century document known as the *Acts of Thomas*, which indicates that Jesus and Thomas looked alike and apparently were close.

∞ 178 ∞

Olive Garden

Before his crucifixion, Jesus went to the Garden of Gethsemane to pray. *Gethsemane* comes from an Aramaic word meaning "oil press." The Garden of Gethsemane today still has many very old olive trees.

∞ 179 ∞

Onesimus

Onesimus was a runaway slave who became a Christian after encountering the Apostle Paul. Paul wanted Onesimus to be on his mission team, so he sent the slave back to his owner, Philemon, with a letter requesting his freedom. The name Onesimus means "profitable," and Paul played with this idea, telling Philemon that even though Philemon once considered him "useless" as a slave, Onesimus had become "useful" in Paul's ministry.

❧ **180** ❧

Luke the Gentile

A comment by Paul in Colossians 4:11 would suggest that Luke was a gentile. That would make him the only known non-Jewish writer of the New Testament.

❧ **181** ❧

Faith and Loyalty

As the future husband of Mary and stepfather of Jesus, Joseph learned of Mary's pregnancy at a unique point in the Jewish premarriage process. They were "betrothed"—a commitment as binding as marriage—but betrothed couples did not yet live together as husband and wife. Nevertheless, it would take a divorce to dissolve a betrothal, and Joseph considered it until an angel visited him in a dream and convinced him to go ahead with the marriage plans.

❧ **182** ❧

A Milestone for Israel

The Romans used distinctive milestones to mark distances on their roads. These were small, round stone columns set on bases by the sides of the roads. The Romans were master engineers, building extensive networks of good roads throughout their empire, along which the Apostle Paul and others traveled. Many milestones are still on Israel's roads today.

183

Papyrus

You probably know that our word "paper" comes from *papyrus*, a plant that grows in marshes and was used as a writing surface in ancient times. But did you know that the inner pith of the papyrus plant was called *byblos*? From this the Greeks got their word for book, *biblion*, from which we got our word "bible."

184

Family Name

Matthew was a former tax collector who became one of the 12 apostles. He wrote one of the four gospels, detailing Jesus' earthly ministry, which became the first book of the New Testament. Mark and Luke both include the story of Matthew's calling, but they refer to him as Levi. This was probably a family surname.

185

The Guilty Set Free

When Jesus was tried before Pontius Pilate, a notorious criminal, Barabbas, was in Roman custody. Pilate failed in his attempt to free Jesus and freed Barabbas instead. Christians have long seen themselves in Barabbas: a guilty man set free because an innocent man died in his place. Appropriately, his name has a generic meaning that could apply to anyone: "son of the father."

∽ 186 ∽

A Lost Ending

The ending to the Gospel of Mark found in English Bibles (Mark 16:9–20) is not found in the earliest surviving manuscripts. Two endings—a shorter ending and the longer one that readers are more familiar with—begin to show up in manuscripts in the fifth century. It is likely that Mark's original ending was lost and that scribes used other available traditions of Jesus' post-resurrection activity to supply what was missing.

∽ 187 ∽

Crossing the Jordan

The Jordan River is famous as the site of Jesus' baptism. Among some believers, the Jordan River has become a symbol for entry into heaven. It is the border one must "cross over" in order to reach the Promised Land.

∽ 188 ∽

The Symbol of the Palm

On Palm Sunday, Christians commemorate Jesus' last entry into Jerusalem, when people placed leafy branches on the path before him. In early Christian art and on Christian tombs, images of palms represented martyrs. Those who died for the faith frequently were portrayed as holding palm leaves. Using traditional symbolism, their victory was shown to be one over death and into newness of life.

❧ 189 ❧

Not the First

The "church" in Corinth consisted of small groups that met in the homes of the wealthier members. Paul sent letters to these house churches, because a number of the converts had difficulty leaving behind their pre-Christian ways. "First" Corinthians was not actually the first letter. Paul makes mention of a previous letter (1 Corinthians 5:9) that occasioned some misunderstanding that he clarifies in this letter.

❧ 190 ❧

The Tentmaker

The Apostle Paul worked as a tentmaker and generally paid his own way, not depending on collections from the congregations he established. Tentmaking was also a great way to meet travelers. If they accepted the gospel, they would spread it.

❧ 191 ❧

Where Is Armageddon?

Revelation 16:16 states that Armageddon is a Hebrew word, but no such word is actually found in Hebrew. Many scholars think it stands for *har-megiddo*, or "mountain of Meggido." Meggido was the site of two decisive battles in the Old Testament, and it might well have served as a symbol of the great final struggle between good and evil.

192

Paul's First Stop in Europe

Macedonia was the first place in Europe that the Gospel was preached. It was a region of northern Greece and was for many years an independent kingdom. Its most glorious period came under Alexander the Great and his father Philip in the fourth century B.C. Paul was moved to preach there by a vision in which a Macedonian man called him to come (Acts 16:9).

193

Home of the Firehouse Dog

From 2 Timothy 4:10, we learn that Titus, one of Paul's companions, had left him to go to Dalmatia. This was a Roman district in what is today Croatia. It is thought to be the original home of the dalmatian breed of dog, the white-with-black-spots firehouse dog.

194

House of Bread

Bethlehem means "house of bread." It is mentioned several times in the Old Testament, most prominently as the city where David was from, but its major importance was as Jesus' birthplace. Many holy sites have sprung up in Bethlehem, although the authenticity of many of them is questionable.

∽ 195 ∽

The Sea of Galilee

This sea is located about 685 feet below sea level, with rugged hills rising abruptly from its eastern and western shores. Its position below sea level and flank of high mountains on the east make it susceptible to severe weather changes and great storms, some of which we read about in the New Testament.

∽ 196 ∽

Earthquakes

The New Testament mentions two earthquakes. One was on the day of Jesus' crucifixion just after he died (Matthew 27:51–53), and the other occurred when Paul and Silas were imprisoned at Philippi (Acts 16:26). This second earthquake broke open the doors of the prison so that the prisoners could have escaped, causing the jailer great distress. Paul and Silas, however, reassured the jailer that everyone was still there.

∽ 197 ∽

Jesus' Footprints?

The Chapel of the Ascension on the Mount of Olives supposedly marks the spot where Jesus ascended to heaven. It was built during Crusader times (in the eleventh century) over a spot marked since the fourth century. A stone slab contains what some claim are Jesus' last footprints on earth.

∞ 198 ∞

Akeldama

Akeldama was the Aramaic name, meaning "field of blood," given to the field bought with the 30 pieces of silver that Judas received when he betrayed Jesus. The name seems to be due to two reasons: the spilling of Judas' blood (Acts 1:18–19), and the fact that the field was bought with "blood money" (from Jesus' betrayal) (Matthew 27:6).

∞ 199 ∞

Where Was Jesus Buried?

Jesus was buried in a rock-cut tomb sealed with a large stone. Many such tombs are known from Jesus' time, with large, circular stones set on edge to cover the entrance. The Garden Tomb near Gordon's Calvary is thought by some to be the site of Jesus' burial, but it is possible the tomb is somewhere under the present-day Church of the Holy Sepulchre.

∞ 200 ∞

The Mount of Olives

The Mount of Olives is a graceful hill just across the Kidron Valley from Jerusalem. Jesus spent much time there in the last weeks of his life. He wept when he saw Jerusalem from it as he returned for the last time, he prayed in the Garden of Gethsemane there, and he was arrested there. It is said Jesus ascended to heaven from the Mount of Olives.

⤬ 201 ⤬

Golgotha

Jesus died at a place called *Golgotha*, which is Aramaic for "skull." Its exact location is disputed. While Gordon's Calvary is a hill with caves, which make it resemble a skull, these caves are artificial excavations only two or three centuries old. Many scholars believe that the present-day Church of the Holy Sepulchre marks the true site of Golgotha.

⤬ 202 ⤬

Jesus before Pontius Pilate

Pilate, the Roman governor of Judea, pronounced judgment on Jesus at a place called the Pavement (in Hebrew, *Gabbatha*) (John 19:13). This was probably in the Antonia, a massive fortress built by Herod which was at the northwest corner of the Temple Mount. Paul was also imprisoned there. A large stone pavement, more than 150 feet square, can be seen today under a convent in this area.

⤬ 203 ⤬

Get Me if You Can!

King Herod fortified Jerusalem by building huge walls and high towers around the city. A three-tower complex defended his palace. The base of one of these towers, named Phasael's Tower, can still be seen today. It is an impressive 60-foot cube, and is popularly, but erroneously, known as David's Tower. It had been 150 feet high.

∽ 204 ∽

Bigger than a Rubik's Cube

In the Apostle John's vision of heavenly Jerusalem (Revelation 21 and 22), he saw a shimmering, bejeweled city descend from heaven. The city was a spectacular fantasy, however, since it was a perfect cube measuring 1,500 miles on each side—the distance from New York to Houston. It was clearly symbolic of the glories that lay ahead.

∽ 205 ∽

Down to Jericho

The good Samaritan is said to have gone down from Jerusalem to Jericho. This doesn't mean that Jericho is south of Jerusalem (it's east), and it doesn't imply that Jericho was a step down from Jerusalem in wealth, urban development, or status. Jericho is 3,300 feet lower than Jerusalem, an amazing drop for a journey of only 15 miles.

∽ 206 ∽

Staying Close to Home

Jesus spent almost all of the first year and a half of his public ministry in the region of Galilee, where he grew up. Many important highways passed through Galilee, going to distant places. Thus, Jesus could have had easy contact with a wide variety of people without traveling very far and without exposing himself early in his ministry to the anger of the religious authorities in Jerusalem.

∞ **207** ∞

Ancient Construction

King Herod was well known for his impressive building projects, like the second temple in Jerusalem. In September 2007, Israeli archaeologists announced the discovery of a quarry within a Jerusalem suburb that had provided Herod with the stones used in his building projects.

∞ **208** ∞

What Was an Apostle?

The Greek word *apostolos* ("apostle") comes from *apostello*, which means "to send." In secular Greek usage, *apostolos* often meant "ship," "fleet," or "naval expedition" (something sent out), but almost never did it mean a person sent. In the New Testament, the meaning was attached to people appointed (or sent) to special functions in the church. Usually it referred to the 12 disciples of Jesus or to Paul.

∞ **209** ∞

The Greeks

In Biblical times, Greece's major contributions were cultural. It contributed a common language for international discourse and developed great traditions of speculative philosophy and republican government. The New Testament was written in Greek, and the Apostle Paul preached in many Greek cities, including Athens.

⤳ **210** ⤦

The Romans

The Roman empire grew to encompass the entire Mediterranean basin during the time of Jesus. Roman contributions were primarily architectural and political. They had a loose provincial system, under which much local autonomy was allowed, and Roman citizens had many rights. The *Pax Romana* ("Roman Peace"), despite its occasional ruthlessness, allowed for the rapid and peaceful spread of the Christian faith in the decades after Jesus lived.

⤳ **211** ⤦

The Cilician Gates

Paul traveled throughout Asia Minor, and he would have seen some spectacular scenery along the way. Near his hometown of Tarsus in southeastern Asia Minor was the Taurus mountain range, which completely blocked off east-west travel. The one route through these mountains was through the Cilician Gates, a deep, narrow pass through wild, rugged terrain.

⤳ **212** ⤦

Simon and "Simony"

The English word "simony" refers to the practice of buying or selling ecclesiastical pardons or offices. It comes from Simon the Magician, who tried to buy spiritual power from the apostles after he saw them laying hands on people and the people receiving the Holy Spirit (Acts 8).

❧ 213 ❧
Beloved Tabitha, the Seamstress

Tabitha, a disciple of Jesus, died in the city of Joppa when Peter was in a neighboring town. Tabitha was loved by the community, as she "was full of good works and charitable deeds" (Acts 9:36). The widows especially missed her, and they showed Peter many of the garments she had made for them. Peter prayed for her, and she was made alive again. Her Greek name was Dorcas; both names mean "gazelle."

❧ 214 ❧
A Ruthless Ruler

King Herod was a ruthless and unpopular ruler who was put in power by the Romans. He executed dozens of political rivals, including a favorite wife and two of his own sons. This same Herod tried to kill the infant Jesus by ordering a mass slaughter of infants in Bethlehem.

❧ 215 ❧
Life of Luxury

Herod's Herodium, 200 feet wide, was a most luxurious place. Seven stories of living rooms, storage areas, and cisterns were built, including a complete Roman bathhouse and a beautiful open courtyard in the area below the top of the walls. It was the third largest palace in the Roman world, and by far the most luxurious in Israel.

❧ 216 ❧

Prophetesses in the New Testament

Several women prophets are seen in the New Testament. Anna was a prophetess (Luke 2:36), and Philip's four daughters prophesied (Acts 21:9). Women were among those who spoke "with other tongues" on the day of Pentecost (Acts 2:1–4), which fulfilled a prophecy of Joel's that "your sons and your daughters shall prophesy" (Joel 2:28).

❧ 217 ❧

The Pharisees

Jesus had many run-ins with Pharisees, especially about the hypocrisy of some. Because of this, "pharisaical" has come to mean hypocritical or sanctimonious. However, the original impulse of the Pharisees was noble: To follow and obey God's Law in every area of life. Unfortunately, this led to a dry and arrogant legalism in some.

❧ 218 ❧

Nicodemus

Nicodemus was a devout Pharisee leader who came to Jesus by night to inquire about Jesus' teachings (John 3). Jesus had an extended discussion with him, and it appears that he became a follower of Jesus while still remaining a Pharisee. Later, Nicodemus defended Jesus in the Sanhedrin, at some risk to his own reputation (John 7:50–52), and he helped to bury Jesus' body (John 19:39–42).

∞ 219 ∞

The Sadducees

Along with the Pharisees, the Sadducees were the major party in Judaism in Jesus' day. They came from a more aristocratic, mostly priestly class, and concentrated more on political affairs than did the Pharisees. They rejected such doctrines as the immortality of the soul, resurrection, or most things having to do with an afterlife.

∞ 220 ∞

A Real Wild Man

John the Baptist, who pointed the way to Jesus and baptized him, lived an ascetic life in the Judean wilderness near the Dead Sea. He survived on simple desert fare, eating whatever the desert provided. His dress was also rustic: He wore a tunic of camel's hair with a leather belt.

∞ 221 ∞

John the Baptist's Mother

Elizabeth was the mother of John the Baptist, descended from "the daughters of Aaron" (Luke 1:5). Her name was the same as Aaron's wife's (Exodus 6:23); its Hebrew form means "my God is (my) oath" (or "one who worships God"). Luke 1:36 states that Elizabeth was Mary's "kinswoman," a general word meaning relative.

∽ **222** ∾

The Essenes

This was an ascetic group of Jews living in Jesus' day who rigorously observed the Sabbath and other Mosaic laws, including ritual purification (although not animal sacrifice). They worked at agriculture and other pursuits, ate in silence, remained celibate, cared for their elderly, and owned all things in common.

∽ **223** ∾

The Zealots

A small minority of Jews in Jesus' day were Zealots—Jewish revolutionaries. They were radical patriots and chafed under pagan Roman rule. They constantly agitated against the Romans, and they were responsible for the revolts that led to the destruction of Jerusalem in A.D. 70. One of Jesus' disciples, Simon the Zealot, had been a member.

∽ **224** ∾

At the Poverty Line

Jesus' family was not wealthy. When his parents brought him to the temple for the purification ceremony 33 days after his circumcision, they offered a sacrifice of two doves or pigeons, in obedience to the law. The normal sacrifice for this ceremony, however, was a lamb. Doves or pigeons were only to be offered by those who could not afford a lamb.

∽ 225 ∾

Salome: Dancer Extraordinaire

Salome was Herod's brother's daughter. She danced for Herod and upon pleasing him, received his promise to do anything for her. She asked for the head of John the Baptist on a plate, a request prompted by her mother (Matthew 14). Rather than be embarrassed in front of his guests, Herod was forced to follow through on Salome's request.

∽ 226 ∾

Jesus' Brothers and Sisters

The Bible mentions Jesus' brothers a number of times and his sisters twice. In two passages, several (or maybe all) of his brothers are mentioned, along with his sisters: "Is this not the carpenter's son? Is not His mother called Mary? And His brothers James, Joses, Simon, and Judas? And His sisters, are they not all with us?" (Matthew 13:55–56). They are also mentioned in Mark 6:3.

∽ 227 ∾

A Prophet without Honor

Early in Jesus' ministry, he had spectacular success, drawing large, appreciative crowds. However, when he went back to his hometown and taught in the synagogue there, people were skeptical. He then said, "A prophet is not without honor except in his own country," and his ministry there was inhibited (Mark 6:4).

∾ 228 ∾

Hated by Jesus

The book of Revelation mentions the doctrine of the Nicolaitans, "which thing I [Jesus] hate" (Revelation 2:15). Nicolaitans were associated with the teaching of Balaam, who encouraged the Israelites to practice immorality and eat food offered to idols. This was in precise violation of an apostolic decree (Acts 15:20).

∾ 229 ∾

Who Were Jesus' Brothers?

Three theories to explain the nature of Jesus' brothers have arisen. One holds that these were stepbrothers, Joseph's children by another marriage. A second holds that they were actually his cousins. A third holds that they were true half-brothers. The first two views preserve a doctrine of the perpetual (lifelong) virginity of Mary, held in the Roman Catholic and Orthodox wings of the church, and the third (held by Protestants) does not.

∾ 230 ∾

Peter the Rock

Peter's name in Greek (*Petros*) means "rock" (*petra*). A climactic point in Jesus' ministry came when Peter confessed that Jesus was the Messiah, the Son of God. Jesus blessed him and said, "You are Peter [*Petros*], and on this rock [*petra*] I will build my church" (Matthew 16:18).

⚬ 231 ⚬

The Bible's Two Sauls

Both men named Saul in the Bible were scoundrels. Saul, the first king of Israel, disqualified himself from being king by his disobedient actions, and he had mental disturbances that caused him to try to kill David several times. Saul of Tarsus was a Jew who persecuted the early Christians. However, he was converted and became the great Apostle Paul!

⚬ 232 ⚬

Peter: Crucified Upside Down?

Christian tradition states that when Peter was martyred, he asked to be crucified upside down, since he was not worthy to be crucified in the same manner as his Lord was. This may not have been an unusual mode of crucifixion. Some evidence suggests that condemned criminals may have had their heels nailed together and their legs hung over the top of the cross.

⚬ 233 ⚬

Pursuers of Virtue

Acts 17:18 mentions Stoic philosophers who argued with Paul at Athens, where they challenged his view of the resurrection of the dead. Paul even quoted a Stoic poet, Aratus, in his argument (Acts 17:28). Stoic philosophy concentrated upon logic, physics, and ethics. Their ethical striving for virtue is their best-known emphasis, in contrast to the Epicureans, who strove to avoid pain.

⟶ **234** ⟵

Priscilla and Aquila

Priscilla and Aquila were Jews from Corinth who were coworkers with Paul. They instructed Apollos, a gifted teacher, in the ways of Jesus, and they provided hospitality for Paul in their home (Acts 18). Priscilla is usually mentioned first, suggesting to some scholars that she played the leading role in the couple's ministry.

⟶ **235** ⟵

Paul's Encourager

Paul had many people who helped and encouraged him in his ministry. One was Onesiphorus, "who often refreshed" Paul. When Paul was imprisoned in Rome, Onesiphorus went to Rome and eagerly looked for him until he found him, where he encouraged Paul greatly. Paul contrasted Onesiphorus' example with that of Phygellus and Hermogenes, who abandoned him and the gospel he preached. (2 Timothy 1:15–18 and 2:17–18)

⟶ **236** ⟵

Which Judas?

Some six different people in the New Testament were named Judas. One was a brother of Jesus (Matthew 13:55) and he wrote the book of Jude. Another Judas was a disciple of Jesus. To distinguish that Judas from Judas Iscariot, John 14:22 calls him "Judas (not Iscariot)."

⊙ **237** ⊙

Paul and Barnabas: Gods?

When Paul and Barnabas when to Lystra (in Asia Minor, present-day Turkey), they healed a lame man. The crowds were so impressed that they called Barnabas Zeus (the lord of all the Greek gods) and Paul they called Hermes (Zeus' son and spokesman for all the gods), since he was the main speaker of the two (Acts 14:12). The people tried to offer sacrifices to them, but the two restrained them from doing so.

⊙ **238** ⊙

A Modest Man

The Apostle John was probably the author of the book of John, but he is not mentioned by name in the book. Instead, he refers to himself as "the disciple whom Jesus loved" or by some other means. For example, he says this about his own witnessing of Jesus' death: "And he who has seen has testified, and his testimony is true, and he knows that he is telling the truth, so that you may believe" (John 19:35).

⊙ **239** ⊙

Joseph of Arimathea

Joseph of Arimathea (a village in Judea) was a wealthy member of the Sanhedrin who came forward and offered his own tomb for Jesus' burial (Luke 23:50–56). He was given Jesus' body and, with help from Nicodemus, wrapped the body and buried it.

❧ 240 ❧
"Render to Caesar"

Some Pharisees tried to trap Jesus by asking him whether they should pay taxes to Caesar. If he said yes, they could accuse him of neglecting God's way. If he said no, he could be accused of subversion of Roman law. Jesus frustrated them by simply showing them a coin with Caesar's likeness on it and stating, "Render to Caesar the things that are Caesar's, and to God the things that are God's" (Mark 12:17).

❧ 241 ❧
The First Christian Martyr

Stephen was a deacon, performed many miracles, and spoke wise words from God. This displeased many Jewish leaders and trumped-up charges were brought against him. He delivered a long indictment of these leaders, accusing them of complicity in Jesus' death. This enraged them so much that they interrupted his speech, dragged him out of the city, and stoned him to death (Acts 6—8).

❧ 242 ❧
A Stupid Question

In Luke 9:51–56, a Samaritan village refused to welcome Jesus and his disciples. James and John were miffed, asking, "Lord, do you want us to command fire to come down from heaven and consume them, just as Elijah did?" What part of "love your enemies" did they not understand?

✆ 243 ✆

Symbolic Numbers

When Peter asked Jesus how many times he should forgive his brother, he probably thought that seven was plenty. Seven symbolized completeness. Jesus, however, replied, "up to seventy times seven" (Matthew 18:21–22). Some translations have "seventy-seven times," but the idea is the same. When you want to make a point with a symbolic number, start multiplying.

✆ 244 ✆

The Hebrew Bible

The Hebrew scriptures have three sections: the Law (*Torah*), the Prophets (*Nabiim*), and the Writings (*Kethubim*). When Jesus talked about "the law and the prophets" in Matthew 5:17, he was using a common phrase of the time that referred to all of the Hebrew scriptures. It's unclear why the third part was left out of that phrase, but it's possible that the Writings were seen as the work of prophets.

✆ 245 ✆

The Tree of Life

Genesis 2:9 describes how God placed a tree called the "tree of life" in the middle of the Garden of Eden as a symbol of eternal life. This same tree is described once again at the end of the Bible. Revelation describes the tree of life growing in the New Jerusalem, bearing 12 kinds of fruit. Its leaves are used for healing (Revelation 22:2).

❦ 246 ❦
Apocalyptic Literature

Puzzled by the book of Revelation? Many modern readers have difficulty with it. What sort of writing was John doing? It was actually a form of writing familiar to John's first readers. From about 200 B.C. to A.D. 100, end times writings appeared which were rich with symbolism. They were tantalizing to read, but difficult to interpret precisely. Scholars refer to this genre as apocalyptic literature.

❦ 247 ❦
The Alpha and the Omega

Eight verses into the book of Revelation, God says, "I am the Alpha and the Omega." *Alpha* and *omega* are the first and last letters of the Greek alphabet. So the Lord was declaring his presence at the beginning and the end of human history. This phrase occurs twice more, uttered by "He who sat on the throne" (God the Father) and by Jesus (Revelation 21:5–6, 22:13).

❦ 248 ❦
Forty Winks

In the Bible, the number 40 represents the development and history of salvation: testing. Jesus fasted in the wilderness for "forty days and forty nights" (Matthew 4:2), and the Bible text plainly records "afterwards he was famished"—which is hardly surprising.

249

Phantom Books

Closing his letter to the Colossians, Paul suggests they swap this epistle with the one he sent to the church in the next town over, Laodicea. However, the Laodicean epistle has been lost to history. In the book of Jude, a strange legend is cited about the archangel Michael arguing with the devil over the body of Moses. Scour the Old Testament, and you won't find that story. It's in a book written between the Testaments, the Assumption of Moses.

250

Precious Stones

About 30 different types of precious stones are mentioned in the Bible. They include multicolored agates, reddish-purple amethysts, green emeralds, red garnets, clear diamonds, shiny pearls, red rubies, and blue sapphires. Revelation describes the New Jerusalem with precious gems lodged in its gates and walls (Revelation 21:18–21).

251

An Exclusive Club

There are more than 2,000 registered saints, two thirds of which are claimed by Italy and France. Among the handful of saints from the United States, Saint Frances Xavier Cabrini, known during her life as Mother Cabrini, was the first American citizen to be canonized by the Roman Catholic Church.

∽ 252 ∽

Rebuilding the "Temple"

The temple that Jesus knew was first built in 516 B.C. It lacked the magnificence of Solomon's Temple, but it was functional. Predicting his own resurrection, Jesus once said he could rebuild the "temple" in three days. His opponents commented, "It has taken forty-six years to build this temple, and will You raise it up in three days?" (John 2:20). Obviously, the symbolism was lost on them!

∽ 253 ∽

A Living Language

By Jesus' day, most Jews in Israel spoke Aramaic, not Hebrew. Those Jews who had scattered throughout the Mediterranean world spoke Greek and local dialects. For 2,000 years, rabbis kept the Hebrew language alive. Then, about 100 years ago, Eliezer Ben-Yehuda, a Lithuanian Jew, worked to revive Hebrew as a spoken language. Modern Hebrew is based upon biblical Hebrew and Talmudic Aramaic, and it has traces of German and Russian.

∽ 254 ∽

Hidden Place

The English word "hell" derives from an old Germanic word meaning "hidden place." Other words for hell in various versions of the Bible include *sheol*, *hades*, and *gehenna*.

255

Educating with Animals

Jesus used animal references in his teachings. During his Sermon on the Mount, he observes, "Look at the birds of the air, for they neither sow nor reap nor gather into barns, yet your heavenly Father feeds them. Are you not of more value than they?" Other animals used in his teachings include dogs and swine.

256

A Nameless Kid

Wherever Jesus went, crowds followed. Once, over 5,000 people gathered to hear him and after a long day were famished. One boy, who had brought a lunch, offered it to Jesus. Jesus used this meager lunch of five loaves of bread and two fish to satisfy the hungry crowd—and there were even leftovers (John 6:1–15)! While the boy was crucial to the story, we never find out his name.

257

Sackcloth

Garments made from the hair of goats, sheep, and camels are often called "sackcloth," which was the clothing of the poor, the powerless, and mourning. In Matthew 3:4–5, John the Baptist wears a camel hair shirt to show his humility and devoutness as he prepares the way for Jesus.

∽ 258 ∾

Run (Naked) for Your Lives!

In Acts 19:11–20, seven young men, who attempted to wield power to exorcise demons, used the names of Jesus and Paul in their incantations over a demonized man. The demon overpowered all of them, telling them that while it knew about Jesus and Paul, it knew nothing of them. Acts reports that the seven exorcists ran from the house naked and bleeding.

∽ 259 ∾

The First "Groupies"

Susanna and Joanna were two women who had been healed by Jesus and took care of day-to-day tasks—laundry, sewing, and cooking—for Jesus and his followers. These women helped to support Jesus and his disciples out of their own means. This would have been scandalous behavior in those days, but they were responding to Jesus' message in a positive, loving way (Luke 8:1–3).

∽ 260 ∾

More Than Metaphor

The book of Revelation isn't all about strange beasts and conflicts. The first few chapters contain messages to specific churches from Jesus. To one church he says: "Behold, I stand at the door and knock. If anyone hears My voice and opens the door, I will come in to him and dine with him, and he with Me" (Revelation 3:20).

⌒ 261 ⌒

Ancient Trash Talk

We often bemoan the lack of manners and discretion in our reality TV age, but the truth is, there have always been crude, loudmouthed, insulting people, even in biblical times. James 4:11 pleads, "Do not speak evil of one another, brethren." And Paul urged the Colossians to "put off all these: anger, wrath, malice, blasphemy, filthy language out of your mouth" (Colossians 3:8).

⌒ 262 ⌒

Biblical Nazareth

In Jesus' time, Nazareth was a very small farming town. In John 1:46, Nathanael responded to Philip's word of Jesus by asking, "Can anything good come out of Nazareth?" Luke describes the town as the site of the Annunciation. It had a significant Jewish population until about A.D. 630, when the Eastern Roman Empire ran them out.

⌒ 263 ⌒

The Last Supper

This was a Passover meal Jesus shared with his disciples on the night he was arrested. From scripture and tradition, the Passover had developed a distinct menu and liturgy, and we see hints of that in the Gospels' account of the Last Supper. Along with Judas, Jesus dips his (unleavened) bread in the dip (which represented the mortar the Israelites used as slaves).

⊙ **264** ⊙

A Vital Profession

Shepherds were important in biblical times, and shepherd imagery is used throughout the Bible. In Luke 2:8–20, angels appear to shepherds tending their flocks at night to announce the birth of Jesus. These shepherds are honored to be some of the first to visit the Christ child. Later, in John 10:11, the adult Jesus tells his followers, "I am the good shepherd. The good shepherd gives His life for the sheep."

⊙ **265** ⊙

The Love of Money

Jesus was tough on the rich, perhaps most famously in Matthew 19:16–24, when a wealthy young man tells Jesus he's been keeping the commandments scrupulously, yet still feels he's lacking something. "Jesus said to him, 'If you want to be perfect, go, sell what you have and give to the poor, and you will have treasure in heaven; and come, follow Me.'" This went over like a lead balloon, and the seeker walked away in frustration.

⊙ **266** ⊙

By the Numbers

The New Testament contains 27 books, 260 chapters, and 7,957 verses. But feel free to count them for yourself, if you have the time!

∞ 267 ∞

Hardy Little Tree

Averaging 26 to 49 feet in height, an olive tree is short and squat—about the size of an apple tree. Though olive trees do not bear fruit until they are 15 years old, they live for hundreds of years; in fact, an olive tree in Algarve, Portugal, has been radiocarbon dated at 2,000 years old. This means that it is possible that there are olive trees in Israel that have been alive since the time of Christ!

∞ 268 ∞

The Marriage Supper of the Lamb

In the rich imagery of Revelation, Jesus is portrayed as the sacrificial Lamb, but at the end of the story, he's very much alive—and he's getting married. The church is described as his bride, and the world ends with a party to end all parties—a reception, if you will. "Blessed are those who are called to the marriage supper of the Lamb" (Revelation 19:9).

∞ 269 ∞

A Prayer for Us

John's Gospel contains a lengthy account of Jesus' teaching and conversation during the Last Supper. He also includes a prayer Jesus prayed at that time. At one point he even prays for us, specifically. "I do not pray for these alone, but also for those who will believe in Me through their word" (John 17:20).

❧ **270** ❧

The Law of Love

At the height of his popularity, Jesus was grilled by interviewers sent by his enemies. "Teacher, which is the greatest commandment in the law?" they challenged. Jesus' reply was brilliant. "You shall love the Lord your God with all your heart, with all your soul, and with all your mind." Then he added—"You shall love your neighbor as yourself"—declaring that all the scriptures hang on these two laws (Matthew 22:36–40).

❧ **271** ❧

A Multitasking Fruit

In ancient Israel, olive oil was used as food, fuel, and as a grooming product. When a host welcomed a guest into his home, he would almost always anoint his head with oil as a sign of respect. Indeed, one of the most famous stories in the New Testament is of Jesus being anointed by an unnamed woman in Mark 14:3–9: "She has done what she could. She has come beforehand to anoint My body for burial."

∽ **272** ∾

The Least of Their Brothers

The lives of the poor, orphaned, elderly, and disabled in ancient Israel were sometimes cruel. Orphans were often used as slaves, and many elderly people did not have relatives. Bible passages like James 1:27 exhort the faithful "to visit orphans and widows in their trouble." And Jesus repeatedly called on his followers to care for one of "the least of these" (Matthew 25:45).

∽ **273** ∾

What Would Jesus Own?

In Jesus' time, Jews were allowed to own property, but all of their possessions could easily be taken away by Roman authorities or taxed. Suffering Hebrews hoped that Jesus might lead a political revolution, but instead, he told them not to collect worldly goods, but rather "store up for yourselves treasures in heaven."

∽ **274** ∾

Common Names

The Bible contains an impressive 33 men named Zechariah, including the father of John the Baptist. There are seven Marys in the New Testament, five men named James, and five men named Judas. Even the name Jesus is found more than once. The thief Pilate releases in place of Jesus was called Jesus Barabbas. And Paul worked with a man named Jesus Justus.

⌘ 275 ⌘

Contractor-Grade Temptation

Jesus' fasting and temptation mainly occurred in the Judean Desert. Satan was in charge of the 40 days of temptation, which began when he tempted Jesus to break his fast by turning rocks into bread. Satan then tried to provoke Jesus to jump from a pinnacle and wait for angels to catch him. Finally, he took Jesus to a mountaintop and tempted him with the kingship of the world. Satan was unsuccessful on all counts!

⌘ 276 ⌘

Frankincense and Myrrh

Frankincense is a resin that was harvested from the tree of the same name; the resin was burned for its rich, pleasant smell. *Myrrh* came from Commiphora trees. Scripture records it as one of the gifts of the wise men at the birth of Jesus and as an embalming agent for him after the Crucifixion—so myrrh would seem special to Christians, as it was part of Christ's birth and death.

⌘ 277 ⌘

The Dead Sea Scrolls

In 1947, some shepherds accidentally found scrolls in a desert cave. Soon archaeologists were going through all the caves in the area, finding more than 800 documents. Many of these are portions of the Hebrew scriptures from about the time of Christ.

∞ 278 ∞

The Lord's Prayer

After criticizing the way hypocrites prayed (showing off) and the way pagans prayed (babbling), Jesus gave his disciples a template: *Our Father in heaven.* This prayer includes praise and petition, confession and commitment. If, as a child, you practiced reciting this prayer as quickly as possible, you missed the point. That would be both showing off and babbling.

∞ 279 ∞

Public Prayer

At the raising of Lazarus, Jesus uttered a rather strange prayer for the benefit of the crowd. He said, "Father I thank You that You have heard me. And I know that You always hear Me, but because of the people who are standing by I said this, that they may believe that You sent Me." (John 11:41–42). This miracle was a demonstration of his identity, and this prayer makes that clear.

∞ 280 ∞

Remarkable Discovery

Timeless treasures often turn up where you least expect them. Such was the case in 2009 and 2010 when Vatican archaeologists discovered the earliest known icons of the apostles Paul and Peter on a ceiling in a catacomb beneath a modern eight-story office building in Rome. The images are believed to date from the second half of the fourth century A.D.

281

Biblical Nicknames

The details of our lives have the potential of earning us "pet" names among our peers and family members. Biblical figures were often given nicknames as well. There was John "the Baptist," Thomas "the Twin," and James and John, who were known as the "Sons of Thunder." And the disciples of Christ, of course, eventually became known simply as "Christians."

282

The Voice of God

Talking to a crowd about his impending suffering, Jesus wondered whether he should ask his Father to avoid it. But he concluded, "But for this purpose I came to this hour..." And then he prayed: "Father, glorify Your name." A voice from heaven replied, "I have both glorified it and will glorify it again." Some thought it was just thunder, but Jesus explained, "This voice did not come because of Me, but for your sake." (John 12:27–30).

∽ **283** ∽

Ancient Drag Racing

In Old Testament times, chariots were commonly used in battle. But by the time Jesus arrived, chariots were no longer used in warfare. Why? Because horses were bred to be bigger and stronger so that warriors could use them alone in battle. However, chariots were still used in Jesus' time for transportation, and chariot races were quite popular.

∽ **284** ∽

Chanukah

Many assume Chanukah to be a Jewish Christmas equivalent. This assumption is false. Although Jews have joyfully celebrated the holiday for more than two millennia since biblical times, it is not even mentioned in the Bible. While scripture does not record Jesus commenting on Chanukah, as a Jew, he likely celebrated it.

∽ **285** ∽

Moved by the Spirit

In Acts 8:26–40, the Spirit told Philip to leave his ministry in Samaria and "go toward the south." When he did, he encountered an Ethiopian official sitting in his chariot puzzling over scriptures. Philip told him about Jesus and baptized him. Then, "when they came up out of the water, the Spirit of the Lord caught Philip away." The evangelist "was found" at another town and continued his ministry.

✆ 286 ✆
Scapegoat

In the Old Testament, the Israelites would sacrifice an animal so humans wouldn't have to pay for their sins in blood. A high priest would sprinkle sacrificial goat's blood on the Ark of the Covenant and then lay hands on the goat to transfer Israel's sin into the "scapegoat." In Romans 3, Paul uses this analogy to explain Jesus' death as atonement "by his blood" for all human sin.

✆ 287 ✆
Jesus: Schoolyard Bully?

The Apocrypha is a collection of dozens of books that have been left out of the official Bible for various reasons. One of these, the Infancy Gospel of Thomas, supposedly describes Jesus' childhood and paints him as a show-off and a vengeful bully. It also alleges that Jesus performed bizarre miracles and killed some boys who had opposed him. Not surprisingly, many biblical scholars believe this book to be a fraud.

✆ 288 ✆
The Root of All Evil

You may have heard that "money is the root of all evil." Not exactly. It's the *love* of money: "For the love of money is a root of all kinds of evil" (1 Timothy 6:10). You can have money, as long as you don't love it.

∽ 289 ∾

An Unfair Label?

It has been a common belief that Mary Magdalene, a devoted follower of Jesus, was a prostitute. However, this idea has been challenged by scholars. The Bible credits Jesus with casting seven demons from her. While most would agree that being rid of demons is a good thing, scripture doesn't elaborate on whether the demons were causing sin or disease.

∽ 290 ∾

Tyre and Sidon

These two Phoenician cities figured briefly in Jesus' ministry. He visited them after straightening out some Pharisees in Genasseret. A woman came to him in Tyre; the disciples tried to brush her off, but the power of her faith convinced Jesus to hear her plea for her daughter. He healed her of a demon before heading back to Galilee. This was his only recorded visit to these cities in the Bible.

∽ 291 ∾

Jesus in Color

Not all comic books star muscle-bound guys in spandex and capes. The 1940s saw a proliferation of biblical comic books, such as The Standard Publishing Company's *The Life of Jesus Visualized*. Subsequent editions included *The Life of Joseph Visualized* and *Parables Jesus Told*. Religious comic books thrived throughout the '50s, '60s, '70s, and '80s.

❧ **292** ❧

No Gentiles Allowed

Only Jews were allowed to pass beyond the outer courtyard of the temple. This restriction, along with a misunderstanding, sparked a riot in which Paul was arrested. He had been seen around town with a gentile friend, and when Paul was spotted later in the temple, his enemies assumed the gentile was with him. People "rushed together" and dragged Paul out of the temple. His arrest by Roman soldiers probably saved his life (Acts 21:27–36).

❧ **293** ❧

Publication of the Apocrypha

In 1820, several books which were left out of the Bible, called the Apocrypha, were collected into a volume called *The Apocryphal New Testament*. It was a kind of alternative to the mainstream Bible. The book was reissued in 1926 as *The Lost Books of the Bible*, and it was reprinted in 1979.

❧ **294** ❧

"Peter's House"

In 1968, the remains of a church were found *underneath* a fifth-century church. The newly discovered church had been built around a private house. The names of Jesus and Peter were found etched in the walls. Some think this was actually Peter's house (where Jesus stayed?), used as a house church, then expanded and built over.

❧ 295 ❧

A Chilling Prophesy

In Luke 21:24, Jesus claims of the Jews that "they will fall by the edge of the sword, and be led away captive into all nations. And Jerusalem will be trampled by Gentiles until the times of the Gentiles are fulfilled." A few decades after Jesus' death, the Romans began the persecution of the Jews that would last for two millennia.

❧ 296 ❧

"Talitha Kum"

A synagogue leader begged Jesus to come to his 12-year-old daughter's deathbed and heal her. By the time Jesus arrived, mourners had assembled, bewailing the girl's death. But Jesus announced that the girl was only sleeping. Some scoffed, but Jesus took her by the hand and said, "Talitha kum"—"little girl, I say to you, arise" (Mark 5:41). Immediately she got up and walked around.

❧ 297 ❧

Be Careful Where You Nap

In Acts 20:9–12, Paul was preaching when a young man named Eutychus fell three stories from a window and died. Fortunately, Paul was able to immediately raise him back to life. But why did Eutychus fall in the first place? The answer is simple: because he fell asleep in the window!

∽ **298** ∾
The Luck of the Draw

Many important decisions in biblical times were made by drawing lots. The sacrificial goat on the Day of Atonement was chosen by lot, and the promised land was apportioned by lot. Achan was revealed by lot as the man responsible for Israel's defeat at Ai, and Saul was chosen Israel's first king by lot. In the New Testament, soldiers cast lots for Jesus' garments, and the disciple who replaced Judas Iscariot was selected by lot.

∽ **299** ∾
Which Day Is Jesus' Birthday?

December 25 was celebrated as the birth date of Jesus by the early fourth century A.D., and probably much earlier. This date was probably selected because the Romans celebrated the Mithraic festival of the sun god on that day, and this was an opportunity to make a pagan festival into a religious one. This date was also near the winter solstice. The Eastern Church celebrates Christmas on January 6. The exact date of Jesus' birth is unknown.

∞ **300** ∞

The Bone-Box of Caiaphas

An errant dump truck did an accidental excavation in Jerusalem in 1990, uncovering an ancient ossuary, or bone-box, belonging to the Caiaphas family. A burial site would be owned by a family, which would collect the bones of ancestors. Dating to the first centuries B.C. and A.D., this bone-box bears the name "Caiaphas" and includes the bones of a 60-year-old male, thought to be the high priest who questioned Jesus.

∞ **301** ∞

Is That Kosher?

In Acts 10, Peter was meditating on a rooftop when the Lord gave him a vision of non-kosher animals. A voice said, "Kill and eat." When he protested, the voice reminded him that *God* decides what's kosher. Just then there were messengers at the door, asking him to preach in the home of a gentile—a "non-kosher" *person*. Peter got the message, and he went with them.

∞ **302** ∞

An Ear to Hear

Jesus did not save his miraculous healing powers only for those who believed in him. Malchus, the servant of the high priest, was with the group of soldiers who came to arrest Jesus. Peter struck him with a sword, severing his ear. But Jesus said, "Permit even this" and healed Malchus' ear. (Luke 22:51)

∞ **303** ∞

Joseph the Stepfather

If anyone gets the short stick in Matthew's genealogy of Jesus, it's Joseph, Jesus' earthly father. Joseph is not called Jesus' father but "the husband of Mary, of whom Jesus was born." This was no doubt written to stress the importance of the virgin birth and the fact that Joseph was not Jesus' biological father.

∞ **304** ∞

Keeper of the Pit

You've heard of the angels Gabriel and Michael, but what about Apollyon? In Revelation, Apollyon is referred to as the angel of the bottomless pit and the king of an army of locusts that appear as fearsome war horses with human faces, lion's teeth, and scalelike breast plates. There has been some debate among theologians as to whether Apollyon is good or evil.

∞ **305** ∞

Bibles in Every Language

Missionary William Cameron Townsend established Wycliffe Bible Translators in 1942, with the goal of translating the Bible into every language in the world. They have their work cut out for them: About 6,900 languages are spoken by the 7 billion people on earth. Only 459 of these languages have decent versions of the Bible, and only 1,213 have adequate New Testaments.

◌ **306** ◌

Satan = Lucifer?

The word *Lucifer* appears only once in the Bible and only in the King James translation. Latin for "light bringer," it is used in Isaiah 14:12 to refer to the king of Babylon and mock his fall from power: "How you are fallen from heaven, O Lucifer, son of the morning!" Because Christians associated this passage with Jesus saying "I saw Satan fall like lightning from heaven" (Luke 10:18), the name Lucifer became another name for Satan.

◌ **307** ◌

The Number 14

When speaking of the genealogy of Jesus, the number 14 has significance. Matthew 1:17 says, "So all the generations from Abraham to David are fourteen generations; from David until the captivity in Babylon are fourteen generations, and from the captivity in Babylon until the Christ are fourteen generations." What's more, each Hebrew letter has a corresponding number, and when the numbers for the name "David" are added up, they equal 14.

∽ **308** ∾

Mistranslation

The Bible is filled with prophetic, poetic, and at times inscrutable prose. Sometimes misinterpretations result in bizarre consequences, such as the formation of the Heaven's Gate and Branch Davidian groups. In fact, there are approximately 5,000 biblical cults in the United States, and approximately 3,000 self-proclaimed "messiahs."

∽ **309** ∾

Who Wrote Hebrews?

Paul is the prime suspect, but Tertullian—who was alive when the original manuscripts were around—referred to Hebrews as the Epistle of Barnabas. Martin Luther guessed that Apollos wrote it. Other nominations are Philip or Priscilla. Clement of Alexandria surmised that Paul wrote it first in Hebrew and then, to account for the excellent Greek, Luke translated it. This might be the best guess of all.

∽ **310** ∾

Martin Luther

Few movements have been as world-changing as the Protestant Reformation. At the heart of it was Martin Luther, haunted by scripture such as Romans 1:17: "The just shall live by faith." Luther believed that righteousness came by faith and not by religious works.

∽ 311 ∾

Divine Inspiration

For hundreds of years, the Bible has inspired some of the most beautiful artwork the world has ever seen. The earliest known biblical paintings date back to around A.D. 70, literally the very beginnings of Christianity, and the earliest sculptures date back to the beginning of the second century A.D. Not surprisingly, much of the earliest biblically themed art depicts events in the life of Jesus.

∽ 312 ∾

Women of the World

Unlike most biblical genealogies, Matthew's genealogy of Jesus includes female descendants: Rahab, Ruth, Bathsheba, Tamar, and Jesus' mother, Mary. Of these five, only one, Mary, was a Jewish woman. The others were gentiles from foreign countries. Matthew may well have been making the statement that Jesus was a Messiah for all people.

∽ 313 ∾

Simple Yet Effective

Jesus' parables may seem familiar today, but in his day, they presented revolutionary ideas using a familiar mechanism. His teachings turned the status quo on its ear. Thus the genius of the method: It imparted radical ideas in ways so simple and accessible we still learn from them today.

∽ **314** ∾

A Good Motto

Puritan colonists in Massachusetts founded Harvard College (later University) in 1636 for education in religion, but also "all good literature, arts, and sciences." The basis for its motto comes from Jesus' words in John 8:32: "And you shall know the truth, and the truth shall make you free."

∽ **315** ∾

Bibles and Bullets

The Bible is great at saving souls, but it has also saved a few lives. In August 2007, a Bible saved the life of PFC Brendan Schweigart when a sniper shot him in Iraq. The bullet embedded itself in the Bible he carried over his heart. And in May 2009, a minister in Argentina was shot by a mugger—but the pastor held up his Bible as the gun went off, and the book's hardcover stopped the bullet.

∽ **316** ∾

Nontrinitarians

Not all Christians believe in the Trinity. Those who don't are called Nontrinitarians, and they have various beliefs of their own. Bitheists believe that the Godhead is composed of two persons—the Father and Son. Ditheists believe that two gods—God and Satan—constantly work against each other. And some Unitarians don't believe in any God at all.

∽ 317 ∾

Working Together for Good

Romans 8:28 says, "And we know that all things work together for good to those who love God, to those who are the called according to His purpose." Too many believers edit this verse to "all things work together for good." When we consider the verse within its chapter, we find that it's far more than a pep talk. It's a powerful truth rooted in God's eternal purposes. The Lord is working on a greater plan—and it's often different from our plans.

∽ 318 ∾

Women's Work

Women do not always feature prominently in the Bible, but Paul had many female associates. Phoebe was a deacon and benefactor, Prisca hosted a church in her house, and Junia spent time with Paul in prison. There was Tryphaena and Tryphosa, "those workers in the Lord," and a hard-working woman named Mary (Romans 16:1–12). Paul acknowledges that Euodia and Synthche struggled beside him (Philippians 4:2–3). And in Philippi, Paul made his headquarters in the home of Lydia, a woman he had baptized.

☙ 319 ❧

The Fifth Gospel?

Christians believe that the promises made in the book of Isaiah were fulfilled in the Gospels. Because of this, Isaiah is often called the fifth Gospel. Jerome, who translated the Bible into Latin in the fourth century, said Isaiah "should be called an evangelist rather than a prophet," because his prophesy was so complete. The New Testament itself is a champion of Isaiah's, citing him 419 times!

☙ 320 ❧

The First Stone

Under Roman occupation, any crime the Romans considered too petty to bother with would be handed over to the local Jewish authorities. Such was the case in John 8:3–7, when the Pharisees brought an adulterous woman to Jesus and asked him what her punishment should be. Jesus replied, "He who is without sin among you, let him throw a stone at her first."

☙ 321 ❧

United We Stand

Abraham Lincoln dealt with the difficulties of a divided country during his presidency. He was also a serious student of scripture, and chose Mark 3:25 as a key text in his efforts to keep the United States united: "And if a house is divided against itself, that house cannot stand."

∽ **322** ∾

The Geneva Bible

Before the King James Version of the Bible, the Geneva Bible was the standard. When Milton or Shakespeare quoted scripture, it was from this version. The language was vigorous and edgy for its day. Amazingly, this was what modern publishers would call a "study Bible," with study guides, maps, and illustrations.

∽ **323** ∾

Another Empty Tomb

The death of Jesus' mother, Mary, is not mentioned in scripture, but she is believed by some theologians to have risen to heaven just as her son did. In fact, her corporeal assumption is a basic tenet of the Catholic Church, because her tomb was empty when it was opened by the disciples following her death.

∽ **324** ∾

Site of Jesus' First Miracle

It's not clear how big Cana was in Jesus' day, but we can assume that it was big enough, at least, to have a major wedding. The simple fact that we can't find the town's ruins, along with its mere three biblical mentions, suggest that it wasn't enormous. It seems reasonable to consider Cana a smallish Galilean town, noteworthy for little except Christ's miracle of turning water to wine.

∽ **325** ∽

A Liberal Translation

In 1768, a prolific writer and creative thinker, Edward Harwood, took the flowery language of eighteenth-century English prose and used it to write his own paraphrase of the New Testament. His rendering of "Thy kingdom come"? "May the glory of thy moral government be advanced, and the great laws of it be more generally obeyed."

∽ **326** ∽

A Desperate Improvisation

In Capernaum, so many people mobbed a house where Jesus was teaching that the door was blocked. When four men arrived with a paralyzed man on a stretcher, they couldn't get in. So they improvised: they took the man up to the roof, cut a hole through the plaster, and lowered the stretcher down to Jesus. Jesus was so moved by this display of faith that he immediately healed the man.

ᘐ **327** ᘐ

Compelling Evidence

It is surprising to learn that there is no concrete archaeological proof that Jesus the man actually existed. However, there is plenty of circumstantial evidence. The letters of Paul in the New Testament were written approximately 20 years after Jesus' death, an incident Paul discusses in detail. There are also records from a historian named Tacitus, who writes about Christians, saying they got their name from a spiritual leader who was executed by Pontius Pilate.

ᘐ **328** ᘐ

Ephphatha—"Be opened"

In Galilee, Jesus encountered a deaf man with a speech impediment. Taking him aside, Jesus put his fingers in the man's ears, and he "spat and touched his tongue." Looking upward, Jesus said something that sounded like "Effatha." The Aramaic word for "open" is *pthah*, and it's passive imperative would have been *ethpthah*. "Immediately his ears were opened, and the impediment of his tongue was loosed, and he spoke plainly" (Mark 7:35).

❧ **329** ❧

A Life Recorded

The Bible isn't the only book which records details of Jesus' life. A Jewish historian by the name of T. Flavius Josephus wrote about him in *The Antiquities of the Jews*, saying, "Now there was about this time Jesus, a wise man, if it be lawful to call him a man, for he was a doer of wonderful works..." Josephus completed this work around A.D. 93–94.

❧ **330** ❧

Did Matthew Write Matthew?

Until the eighteenth century, Matthew was the unquestioned author of the Gospel of Matthew. But today, most scholars believe Matthew was written by an anonymous Jewish Christian. Many of Matthew's passages incorporate entire sections of Mark, and the book was written in eloquent Greek. Few people could write in a nonnative language at this time.

❧ **331** ❧

Lamb of God

In the Gospel of John, Jesus is referred to as "the lamb of God who takes away the sin of the world." The exact meaning of this phrase has caused much debate among biblical scholars. Some believe John saw Jesus as a symbolic sacrificial lamb for the atonement of all sins, while others believe he may have been referring to the horned ram that led a flock, the traditional symbol of the king of Israel.

✑ 332 ✑

The Trinity

The idea of the Trinity is based upon passages such as Matthew 28:19, which says, "Go therefore and make disciples of all the nations, baptizing them in the name of the Father and of the Son and of the Holy Spirit." While neither Matthew nor any of the apostles ever say that these three exist as one, most mainstream Christian theologians believe the implication is obvious.

✑ 333 ✑

Which John?

The prophetic author of Revelation calls himself "John to the seven churches that are in Asia," and is assumed by most scholars to be the apostle John. However, some theologians disagree with that assumption, suggesting instead that the author may actually have been a disciple of John.

✑ 334 ✑

All Are Welcome

A common presumption is that Christianity built its early base through appeal to the vast Roman lower classes. In reality, however, this was not true. Scriptural descriptions of the early Christian church's membership, though sketchy, refer to a variety of social classes. While not many early Christians were wealthy, that was true of overall Roman demographics.

335

Home Base

Since his steps took him across the Galilee countryside quite often, Jesus did much of his teaching on the way from one town of Galilee to another: Cana, Tiberias, Nazareth, Capernaum. All his walks along the western shore of the Sea of Galilee passed through the Galilean fishing villages where he performed some of his best-known miracles. Very probably, Jesus knew Galilee the way you know your own home county.

336

The Answer Is No

The apostle Paul had a problem. He called it a "thorn in the flesh," but we're not sure what it was. He asked God three times to remove the problem, but that didn't happen. Finally, God responded, "My grace is sufficient for you, for My strength is made perfect in weakness" (2 Corinthians 12:9). It's a great lesson for all of us: God does answer prayer, but sometimes the answer is no.

⊶ **337** ⊷

Cast of Characters

Like any good story, Revelation features several compelling characters. These include a heroic Jesus; his adversary, Satan (who is referred to by many names in Revelation, including "the dragon," "the Beast," and the "False Prophet"); the archangel Michael; the Four Horsemen of the Apocalypse; and the Whore of Babylon, who is not a woman, but rather a reference to Rome.

⊶ **338** ⊷

What Did Angels Look Like?

Angels are regularly described in the Bible as beings of light. Sometimes they look like men in bright clothing. And people are usually terrified to see them: the angel Gabriel told both Zechariah and Mary not to be afraid of him. Some angelic beings, like cherubim and seraphim, have wings, but it's not certain that all angels which appear in the Bible did.

⊶ **339** ⊷

Chronologically Challenged

If you've ever tried to read the Bible like a novel, you've probably been disappointed. It is not meant to be read as one continuous story, but rather as a collection of different types of literature with one theme. The New Testament follows this outline: The Four Gospels, Early Church History, The Apostle Paul's Letters to the Churches, General Letters, and Revelation.

∾ **340** ∾

Merry X-mas

During the Christmas season, "Merry X-mas" is a greeting frequently seen on gifts, cards, and signs. Some critics of this expression see it as heretical, seeing it as a way to take Christ out of Christmas. However, the X in this expression refers to the Greek letter *chi*, which is the first letter in the Greek word that we translate as "Christ."

∾ **341** ∾

Sacrificial Lamb

Blood represented life in the Bible, and shed blood represented death. The sacrifice for sin required the shedding of blood. This was true whether the victim was an innocent animal or the ultimate sacrificial lamb, Jesus. Because of its special significance, Jews were to drain blood from meat before eating it. This is required for a kosher diet.

∾ **342** ∾

End to the Devil

The book of Revelation describes a future war between God and Satan, in which the devil loses and is imprisoned for a thousand years. He then returns to power, but God again defeats him, and the devil is "cast into the lake of fire and brimstone" where he "will be tormented day and night forever and ever" (Revelation 20:10). Even through Revelation's confusing imagery, one thing is clear: God triumphs over evil.

∽ 343 ∽

Jesus and John the Baptist

We only know fragments of the relationship between Jesus and John the Baptist. Their mothers were cousins, but they grew up in separate towns, with a four-day walk between them. The gospels give us only a few direct interactions between the men, but they were obviously aware of each other. At one point, Jesus declared of John, "Assuredly, I tell you, among those born of women there has not risen one greater than John the Baptist" (Matthew 11:11).

∽ 344 ∽

Famous Last Words

While on the cross, Jesus cried, "*Eli, Eli, lema sabachthani?*" This is Hebrew for, "My God, my God, why have you forsaken me?" Some bystanders thought he was calling for Elijah; however, this is actually the first verse of Psalm 22, which contains an eerily accurate description of the process of crucifixion (though it was written centuries before the Romans invented crucifixion).

☙ 345 ☙

Raising the Dead

Jesus performed many miracles, including restoring sight to the blind, feeding thousands with a handful of food, and walking on water. But perhaps his most astounding miracle was the resurrection of the dead. He did this three times, according to the Gospels: the daughter of Jairus, a young man from Nain, and Lazarus, a close friend who had been dead for four days.

☙ 346 ☙

Faith vs. Works

Martin Luther embraced the biblical explanation of salvation found in the Gospels—a relationship with God by grace through faith in Christ's work. But the book of James states that a person is justified by works and not by faith alone. Luther dubbed James a "gospel of straw" because of its emphasis on works. However, the book was simply explaining that good works flow out of real faith.

☙ 347 ☙

No Limit

Paul had a special love for the church in Ephesus, where he spent over two years. We see his affection in the poetic prayer included in Ephesians 3:14–21. He wanted them to be "rooted and grounded in love," to know "the width and length and depth and height" of Christ's love, which "passes knowledge."

☙ **348** ☙

Guided by the Spirit

The Holy Spirit appears throughout the Bible. Paul describes two important activities of the Holy Spirit—the gifts of the Spirit and the fruits of the Spirit. Every believer has at least one special ability granted by the Spirit for the glory of God. (1 Corinthians 12:7–11). And when a believer is guided by God's Spirit, the resulting "fruit" is love, joy, peace, patience, kindness, generosity, faithfulness, gentleness, and self-control. (Galatians 5:22–23)

☙ **349** ☙

No Gentiles Allowed

Only Jews were allowed to pass beyond the outer courtyard of the Temple, the Court of the Gentiles. Warning signs in Greek and Latin were posted at regular intervals forbidding others to enter, on pain of death. The book of Acts records a near riot when Jews thought that the Apostle Paul had taken one of his Greek friends into the inner courtyards. Two such notices, engraved on limestone blocks, have been found.

∽ **350** ∽
An Effort to Be Loyal

Jesus had predicted that the disciples would scatter, and Peter contradicted him: "Even if all are made to stumble, yet I will not be" (Mark 14:29). That might explain why Peter followed Jesus at least as far as the courtyard: "But Peter followed Him at a distance to the high priest's courtyard" (Matthew 26:58).

∽ **351** ∽
Humpty Dumpty and the Apostle Paul

In a famous passage in Lewis Carroll's *Through the Looking Glass,* Humpty Dumpty says, "When I use a word, it means just what I choose it to mean—neither more nor less." The Apostle Paul wasn't quite this cavalier, but he did take certain Greek words and give them new meanings or nuances. This was often necessary because classical Greek did not have ways of expressing the great theological truths he wanted to explain.

∽ **352** ∽
First to Hear the Good News

Why were shepherds the first to hear of Jesus' birth? Perhaps they were told because they represented the common people; they were not kings or military leaders. Perhaps they were told because Jesus himself would come to be understood as a shepherd, or because King David had been a shepherd. Or perhaps they were told just because the angels wanted to share the news with those close by.

☙ 353 ❧

Prophesy Fulfilled

Christians believe that Jesus' death in the New Testament was predicted in the Old Testament. Zechariah refers to his betrayal by a friend, specifying the price of 30 silver shekels. Other passages foretell his silent conduct and acceptance of his fate at trial. And Isaiah 53 gives a vivid description of a divine servant sent to endure suffering, abuse, and death.

☙ 354 ❧

The Baptism of Jesus

Jesus' ministry did not begin in the temple or synagogue or within the capital city of his day. Instead, he traveled to the Jordan River, where he was baptized by his cousin John. What may stand out the most about Jesus' baptism is not who was involved or where it was done. What stands out the most is a clear sense of call and appointment of Jesus of Nazareth.

☙ 355 ❧

Dining with Traitors

In ancient Israel, tax collectors were considered traitors by their fellow Jews. That is why Jews were so appalled at Jesus' casual attitude toward taxes. He also socialized with tax collectors. One of them, a man named Zacchaeus who had been skimming from the taxes he collected, repented of his ways after Jesus dined in his home.

∽ 356 ∽
Exiled to Patmos

The first chapter of Revelation states, "I, John . . . was on the island that is called Patmos for the word of God and for the testimony of Jesus Christ" (Revelation 1:9). Patmos was one of several Aegean islands used by the Romans for exile, especially for soothsayers and prophets. If John talked about his Revelation visions before his exile, it would explain why he was sent to Patmos.

∽ 357 ∽
Lydia

Lydia was a merchant from Thyatria, and she sold purple cloth. She is described as a "worshipper of God," identifying her as a Gentile who was attracted to Judaism. When she met Paul, she was living in Philippi and was attending a prayer meeting with other women by the river. After listening to what Paul had to say, she became the first European convert to Christianity.

∽ 358 ∽
James: Faith in Action

Whereas Romans, Galatians, and Hebrews stress the importance of faith alone in one's relationship to God, the book of James presents the case that faith without good works to demonstrate this faith is dead intellectualism.

∞ 359 ∞

Jesus' Blasphemy?

In the course of a debate with a group of Jews, Jesus claimed to have seen Abraham. When they challenged this statement, he replied, "before Abraham was, I AM" (John 8:58). The Jews were enraged with this reference to "I am," since only God was to be referred to in this way. They considered this blasphemy, and tried to stone Jesus to death. This is one of the most direct statements in the Gospels equating Jesus with God.

∞ 360 ∞

Jesus' Tunic

Why did the Roman soldiers at Jesus' crucifixion cast lots for his tunic? According to John 19:23, Jesus' tunic "was without seam, woven from the top in one piece." Most looms of Jesus' time produced cloth that was about three feet wide, so two panels had to be sewn together to make a tunic. But the looms in Galilee were wide enough to weave a tunic in one piece, making Jesus' seamless tunic more valuable.

◌ 361 ◌

INRI: Jesus of Nazareth, King of the Jews

All four Gospels state that a plaque was placed on Jesus' cross identifying him. John states that it was written in Hebrew, Latin, and Greek. The letters "INRI," often seen on this plaque in paintings of Jesus' crucifixion, represent the Latin words for the phrase, "Jesus of Nazareth, King of the Jews."

◌ 362 ◌

Jerusalem

This ancient city has a history stretching back 6,000 years. By Jesus' time, the city had been conquered numerous times and had been under Roman rule since 63 B.C.

◌ 363 ◌

Blood Money

When Judas Iscariot betrayed Jesus to the Jewish authorities, Judas was given 30 pieces of silver in payment. This has led to the phrase "blood money," which is money received in exchange for the life of a human being.

❧ **364** ❧

Objects of Affection

A mulets, like crucifixes, have been around since biblical times. During the Reformation, men like Martin Luther and John Calvin raged against them as a form of idolatry. They preached the doctrine of *sola scriptura*, the belief that the words of the Bible were all any person needed to lead a holy life.

❧ **365** ❧

No Microphone Needed

S ome scholars believe Jesus gave his Sermon on the Mount atop a hill on the north end of the Sea of Galilee that acts as a natural amphitheater. Voices are naturally amplified there, so Jesus, speaking in a normal voice, could easily have been heard as far as 200 yards away.